PICTURING MINNESOTA

1936-1943 Photographs from the Farm Security Administration

Edited with text by ROBERT L. REID

MINNESOTA HISTORICAL SOCIETY PRESS ☐ St. Paul ☐ 1989

Publication of this book was supported in part by the Minnesota Historical Society Public Affairs Center, which is funded by the Northwest Area Foundation.

Minnesota Historical Society Press
St. Paul 55101

Manufactured in the United States of America
10 9 8 7 6 5 4 3 2 1

This publication is printed on a coated paper manufactured on an acid-free base to ensure its long life.

International Standard Book Number:
0-87351-247-2 Cloth
0-87351-248-0 Paper

Library of Congress Cataloging-in-Publication Data

Picturing Minnesota, 1936–1943 : photographs from the Farm Security Administration / edited with text by Robert L. Reid.
    p.   cm.
    ISBN 0-87351-247-2 (alk. paper) : $35.95 — ISBN 0-87351-248-0 (pbk. alk. paper) : $19.95
    1. Minnesota — Description and travel — 1858–1950 — Views.
    2. Minnesota — Social life and customs — Pictorial works.   I. Reid, Robert L., 1938–   . II. United States. Farm Security Administration.
    F607.P53   1989
    977.6'052'0222 — dc20   89–13104
                                                         CIP

OPPOSITE: The Yankoski children ready to leave for school in an old wagon. Beltrami Island reforestation project. July 1936.
Paul Carter

PICTURING MINNESOTA
1936–1943

One of the McRaith grandchildren. Meeker County. February 1942. *John Vachon*

CONTENTS

PREFACE

THIS ALBUM of Minnesota photographs takes us back to the years of the Great Depression and World War II, an era when the American people faced monumental challenges. Perhaps the most evocative records of this national response are the more than 200,000 images taken by a group of photographers who worked for the federal government. These men and women, employees of the Historical Section of the Farm Security Administration (FSA), documented the daily activities of Americans in the midst of domestic uncertainty and international conflict.

I was privileged to review the entire set of Minnesota photographs housed in the Prints and Photographs Division of the Library of Congress in Washington, D.C. At least 1,500 captioned prints were taken in Minnesota, of which 171 appear here. With the help of Jean A. Brookins and Alan Ominsky of the Minnesota Historical Society Press, I selected the images that best illustrate the responses of Minnesotans to the problems they faced some fifty years ago. Although the photographs could be grouped in several ways (by photographer, geography, or chronology, for example), I chose to focus attention, as the photographers did, on social and economic activity, with special emphasis on the ways in which people earned a living. As a Minnesota-born historian interested in the twentieth century, I have also tried to present images reflecting the insights of John Vachon (1914–75), a native of St. Paul and a key member of the FSA staff. Writing about 1939, Vachon noted that the FSA photographer needed both understanding and feelings:

Despite the fact that he is going to use an impersonal instrument to record what he sees, yet he must be intelligent enough to place what he sees in a true perspective of the American scene, to feel the humorousness, the pity, the beauty of the situation he photographs. . . . The photographer must have an impelling desire to record what he sees and feels. He will want to freeze instantaneously the reality before him that it may be seen and felt by others. ("Standards of the Documentary File," Roy E. Stryker Collection, University of Louisville Photographic Archives, Louisville, Kentucky)

I wish to thank the many people who helped make this book possible. Librarians and media specialists at the Library of Congress, the National Archives, the University of Louisville Photographic Archives, the Minnesota Historical Society, and the University of Southern Indiana provided essential assistance as I conducted my research. I am especially indebted to Beverly W. Brannan and Leroy Bellamy at the Library of Congress, James C. Anderson and David Horvath at the University of Louisville, and Jean Brookins, Alan Ominsky, Deborah L. Miller, and Elaine H. Carte at the Minnesota Historical Society. I am grateful to Jack Delano and Gordon Parks for sharing information about their experiences as members of the FSA project and its successor agency, the Office of War Information.

Minnesotans who helped with my research include Mrs. Ralph Aakhus, Effie; Mr. and Mrs. Robert H. Classon, Minneapolis; Mr. and Mrs. Wayne Classon, Plymouth; Harold

Curb, Gemmell; Leonard Dickinson, Bemidji; Mrs. Ruth Elkins, a native of Red Wing now living in Washington, D.C.; Daryl W. Franklin, William Milbrath, and Dick Stivers, Austin; Dr. David Lothner, Duluth; Michael McRaith, Winsted; Mr. and Mrs. Patrick McRaith, Meeker County; Dana Miller, Iron Range Research Center, Chisholm; Carroll Nelson, Litchfield; Theodore A. Norelius, Lindstrom; Don Riley, St. Paul; and Ben Thoma, Willmar.

Martha Barrows and Michele Yonts typed the manuscript, and Sandra Hermann provided editorial assistance. My wife, Joanne, and children, Erik and Kristin, are Minnesotans in spirit who understood the restrictions placed on family life during the preparation of the text and the selection of the photographs. My special thanks go to two members of John Vachon's family—his brother Robert and his daughter Ann. These delightful people not only shared their personal recollections of John, but they also allowed me to use the rich and extensive correspondence that he wrote to his mother, Ann, and to his wife, Penny.

Vachon and his colleagues were outstanding photographers, but the willing cooperation of the many Minnesotans who allowed their pictures to be taken was a crucial element in the photographers' success. Without these people, often unidentified in the captions, there would be no book. They include the young boy featured on the cover, now Bishop John McRaith of Owensboro, Kentucky, whose family owned the Meeker County farm where Robert Vachon worked in the summers. The McRaiths were the subjects of John Vachon's cameras during visits in 1940 and 1942. The continuing enthusiasm of Robert Vachon and the McRaiths for the FSA project reinforced my own appreciation of the significance of these photographs, important historical documents that help us to picture life in Minnesota during a difficult period.

The photographs are presented with their original captions, which were written by the FSA staff in Washington, D.C., from notes supplied by the photographers. A few captions have been shortened, and some have been corrected for punctuation, spelling, and capitalization. Corrections of fact are shown in brackets, as are minor additions. Negative numbers are listed on page 199 to help readers locate photographs in the Prints and Photographs Division of the Library of Congress.

INTRODUCTION

☐ JOHN VACHON left his home in the suburban Washington, D.C., community of Greenbelt, Maryland, on January 24, 1942, the trunk and back seat of his 1937 Plymouth sedan loaded with clothing, books, film, and cameras. A native of Minnesota, he worked for an obscure government agency known as the Historical Section of the Farm Security Administration (FSA). His wife, Millicent (Penny), and their two young children remained behind. For the next six months Vachon traveled across the United States taking photographs of a nation at war.[1]

The pictures taken by Vachon became part of an extensive collection of photographs now housed in the Library of Congress. Known as the FSA-OWI (Office of War Information) Collection, the set includes some 107,000 captioned prints and 210,000 negatives taken between 1935 and 1943. Edward Steichen, one of America's most respected photographers, praised the photographs in the FSA-OWI Collection as "the most remarkable human documents that were ever rendered in pictures." Reflecting on his distinguished career, John Vachon described the work of the Historical Section as the "most monumental" photography project ever conceived.[2]

The creative genius behind the FSA-OWI project was Roy Emerson Stryker, who went to Washington in the summer of 1935 to head the Historical Section of the Resettlement Administration. President Franklin D. Roosevelt had created the agency by executive order earlier that year and had named Rexford Guy Tugwell, an economics professor who was one of his close advisors, as its administrative head. Stryker had been Tugwell's student and then his colleague in the economics department at Columbia University. During the 1920s Tugwell, Thomas Munro, and Stryker co-authored an innovative textbook entitled *American Economic Life and the Means of Its Improvement*. This book, which made extensive use of photographs selected by Stryker, helped to develop his strong interest in visual images.[3]

By the time Stryker went to Washington, the major New Deal farm legislation — the Agricultural Adjustment Act of 1933 — had helped to stabilize farm prices and improve conditions for established farmers in the wake of the hardship brought on by the Great Depression. The Resettlement Administration coordinated government programs that addressed the problems of rural people who were chronically impoverished. Tugwell, who also served as undersecretary of agriculture, was particularly concerned with those in the lower third of the population whom President Roosevelt described in his second inaugural address as "ill-housed, ill-clad, and ill-nourished." In the countryside these were tenant farmers, sharecroppers, migrant workers, and hired hands.

Although the Historical Section was authorized to support the work of researchers, statisticians, economists, and sociologists, Stryker's unit concentrated on photography from the beginning. This decision was not surprising. By the 1930s, photography had become one of the most popular features of American life. "Many [Americans] felt compelled to take photos," noted two historians of the period, "and nearly everyone felt compelled to look at them." The FSA-OWI project was unique because Stryker understood that the camera could

Dawson. February 1942. *John Vachon*

record American history. To achieve this goal, he hired professional photographers who went beyond the collection of file photographs of rural relief and land use projects to a broad look at virtually all aspects of American life. Stryker and Tugwell saw documentary photographs as learning aids that would help enlighten the American people and arouse the conscience of the nation.[4]

Within two years Tugwell left the federal government. His term had been controversial, reflecting mounting criticism of the Resettlement Administration's rural rehabilitation, resettlement, and land use programs. In 1937 Congress renamed the agency the Farm Security Administration and placed it under the Department of Agriculture. The FSA continued its concern for the rural poor, but the emphasis shifted to the rehabilitation of established farm families through assistance in the form of loans and expert advice.[5]

The work of the Historical Section mirrored this shift in policy. Early photographs dramatized the need for government assistance by featuring poor farmers and poor land. In 1938, with the major New Deal measures designed to alleviate the worst problems of the depression in place, Stryker instructed new staff photographer Marion Post to "show something other than the 'lower third' of the country." By this time Stryker's project was covering life in cities and small towns, as well as on the farm. Jack Delano, who joined the staff in 1940, captured the essence of the FSA-OWI photographic project when he called it "a search for the heart of the American people."[6]

The Historical Section narrowed its focus as the nation eased out of the depression and moved toward war. Selective service began in September 1940, and FSA photographers increasingly used their cameras to record defense activities. Two years later the Office of War Information officially absorbed Stryker's agency; accordingly, its task became the documentation of the nation's prosperity and military strength. The reduced staff was sent to photograph war industries and related home-front scenes, images that were intended primarily for propaganda purposes at home and abroad. Stryker, increasingly discontented with the restrictions placed on his photographers, left the government in the fall of 1943 to head a documentary photography project for Standard Oil of New Jersey. Before leaving he arranged the transfer of the FSA-OWI files to the Library of Congress, thereby assuring their accessibility for future generations.[7]

Although other New Deal agencies documented their work through photography, none left a legacy that compares to that of the FSA Historical Section. Stryker's use of outstanding professionals who brought a breadth of vision to their work made the FSA-OWI project truly unique. He hired Arthur Rothstein, one of his former undergraduate students who had a passion for cameras, as his first staff photographer. Rothstein, who documented in photographs virtually every aspect of the early days of the agency, set up the laboratory and was one of the first to go into the field. His work in Minnesota included a 1936 series from Itasca State Park at the headwaters of the Mississippi River. Later he took pictures at a farm near Farmington as part of a series on corn that was shot primarily in Iowa. In 1940 Rothstein joined the staff of *Look,* a new photo magazine that, along with *Life,* was founded soon after the creation of the Historical Section; he served for many years with distinction as senior photography editor.[8]

Paul Carter, another FSA photographer, visited Minnesota a few weeks before Rothstein's assignment at Itasca. In the summer of 1936 he covered two early New Deal projects in the state, the Beltrami Island Settler Relocation Project and Austin Acres. The first attempted to relocate families in the sparsely settled region of northern Minnesota that was part of the impoverished Great Lakes Cutover region; the other provided suburban housing for workers in a town dominated by the meat-packing plant of George A. Hormel and Company. Carter's images of the Yankoski family in northern Minnesota illustrated the difficulties of bringing essential services such as education to people in a poor and isolated area. But most of his work, as in the scenes at Austin Acres, lacked imagination. With Stryker's encouragement, he left the Resettlement Administration soon after his return from Minnesota.[9]

Dorothea Lange and Walker Evans, the best known of the photographers who worked for the FSA, both joined the Historical Section with established reputations. Lange, who was known for her strong images depicting migrants from the region of the Great Plains known as the Dust Bowl who were seeking opportunity in California, covered the West Coast for Stryker. Evans's images of the rural poor in the South were taken with meticulous care. As the FSA photographs taken by Lange and Evans were used by news bureaus and government publications, the quality of the work of the Historical Section achieved wide recognition. Soon the pictures were featured in major exhibits that presented photography as an art form.[10]

Although neither Lange nor Evans took photographs in Minnesota, their influence on John Vachon helped to shape the Minnesota file. When Stryker was setting up his office and hiring his staff in the summer of 1935, Vachon was leaving home, hitchhiking to Washington, D.C., to begin study in English literature at Catholic University of America. A graduate of the College of St. Thomas in St. Paul, he was twenty-one years old and away from home for the first time. Vachon completed a semester of graduate study before his dismissal for violating school rules against drinking. Rather than return home he decided to stay in Washington, enlisting the support of Minnesota Democrats in finding a government position. Despite his hopes for a job at the Library of Congress, Vachon accepted an invitation to be interviewed by Stryker for a temporary position at the Historical Section. The applicant, at that time showing no interest in photography, joined the section as "assistant messenger" in May 1936 and was given a permanent position in July. His initial assignment was to write the caption and photographer's name on the back of each eight-by-ten-inch print, but soon he became the major person responsible for the organization and use of the FSA files.[11]

Through his work he came to "know one photographer's work from another." "Sometimes my work gets interesting," he wrote home to his mother. "I see photographs of all sorts of people in all parts of the country." He said years later that he came "under the influence of Walker Evans, Ben Shahn, Dorothea Lange, and to a lesser degree, Arthur Rothstein, and Russell Lee."[12] Stryker, the teacher, noticed Vachon's growing enthusiasm and encouraged his clerk to borrow a camera. Armed with a thirty-five-millimeter Leica, Vachon took photographs in and around Washington on weekends with his wife-to-be Penny Leeper in the spring of 1937. He described this new interest to his mother:

> I never thought anything could get me like I've been got the past few weeks. I think I've got it for the rest of my life. Saturday and Sunday I took 36 pictures with a $250 camera. They all came out well. I think Stryker is going to put some of them in the files. When he saw them he said, "Well John, it looks like we'll have to get someone else to take care of the file."

He ended his letter by saying: "It may be my life work."[13]

Stryker did put Vachon's photographs into the collection, but several years would pass before he completely relieved the new photographer of his responsibility for the files. Instead Vachon worked on field assignments that became more frequent and longer in duration. He moved from early attempts to imitate Evans (who insisted that he learn to use a clumsy eight-by-ten-inch view camera) to the development of his own style, "always looking for the good picture." Vachon gave the credit to Stryker, saying that "he made a photographer out of me."[14] As his assignments in the field grew, he included Minnesota in his work. When he went home to visit his parents, Ann and Harry Vachon, and his boyhood friends in St. Paul, his cameras accompanied him. In September 1939 he photographed the Twin Cities, the small towns of west-central Minnesota, and northern Minnesota. The next year he took pictures in Minneapolis and St. Paul and also photographed a farm family, the McRaiths, who lived in Meeker and Wright counties. In 1941, as a full-time photographer, he covered Duluth, the iron ranges, the Hormel plant in Austin, and a variety of work-related activities in the Twin Cities. His last major assignment in 1942 included a return visit to the McRaith family and a series on farmers registering for selective service.

Vachon left the agency along with Stryker in 1943 to become a photographer for the Standard Oil project. Only his boss served the Historical Section for a longer time. After the war Vachon spent a year on a photographic assignment for the United Nations Relief Fund, rejoining Stryker at Standard Oil in 1947. A few months later his former colleague, Arthur Rothstein, hired him as a staff photographer for *Look* magazine. He held this position until *Look* ceased publication in 1971, when he became a free-lance artist. When John Vachon died in 1975, his prediction to his mother some thirty-eight years earlier had been fulfilled: photography had indeed formed his life's work.[15]

Russell Lee, who was trained as a chemical engineer, joined the staff in 1936 following an earlier career as the manager of a paint factory. Born in Ottawa, Illinois, Lee was independently wealthy and thus had the freedom to shift his employment. He left the business world to pursue a career in art in 1929, eventually finding photography to be his best medium of expression. Lee took more photographs and spent more time in the field than any of the other FSA photographers. His patience, enthusiasm for the work, and love for detail made him the "ideal FSA photographer," in the words of a later commentator.[16]

Lee left Washington on assignment in October 1936 and did not return until the following summer. He photographed tenant farmers in Iowa and the aftermath of the Great Ohio River Flood of 1937 in Illinois and Indiana before traveling north to the distressed cutover region. His Minnesota images include lumbering, iron mining, the sugar beet harvest in the Red River valley, and blueberry picking by Ojibway Indians. He also took scenes of people down on their luck in Minneapolis and of Mexican Americans in St. Paul. Lee's photographs of the Twin Cities, when combined with those of Vachon, provide one of the most extensive sets of urban materials in the FSA-OWI files. Lee left the FSA-OWI project in 1942 to join the Army Air Transport Command. After the war he served on Stryker's staff at Standard Oil until that project ended in 1950. He spent the rest of his career as a free-lance photographer and as a teacher at the University of Missouri and the University of Texas at Austin.

Three other photographers contributed to the Minnesota file. Marion Post Wolcott, a former newspaper photographer, had become a member of the FSA staff in 1938. She took several pictures in Minnesota as she traveled to Montana in 1941. She described Wisconsin and Minnesota as "beautiful and interesting" and hoped that her pictures of grain elevators "sticking up out of much space" would be successful.[17] Two excellent images of these structures, one taken in Minneapolis and the other in Sauk Centre, appear in this book, as well as a scene of fields near Fergus Falls. Wolcott's photographs tend to reflect the more optimistic story of an America emerging from the worst of the depression.

Jack Delano was an experienced commercial photographer when he joined the staff as a replacement for Rothstein in 1940. Stryker described him as an artist who would ask, "What is the one picture I can take that will say Vermont?"[18] The OWI sent him to Minnesota in 1942 to document Swedish Americans in pictures that were intended for propaganda related to neutral Sweden. His assignment centered in Chisago County, where he captured the determination of people who were experiencing war on the home front.

The other person who took photographs for the Minnesota file was Roy Stryker. Maybe to protect himself from critics — including his own photographers — Stryker distanced himself from the work of his staff. "Perhaps my greatest asset was my lack of photographic knowledge," he once said.

> I didn't subscribe to anybody's particular school of photographic thought. I had what was then a strange notion — that pictures are pictures regardless of how they are taken.
> I was never a photographer. I was a teacher and gadgeteer. I always had a camera but I had no more business with that damn Leica than with a B-29. I got a hell of an inferiority complex because of it. My aunt and I once shot a family reunion. Her ten-dollar Brownie got everything while I drew blanks. I never snapped a shutter after that.[19]

One of Stryker's assistants, Edwin Rosskam, confirmed this evaluation. In the afterword to Sherwood Anderson's *Home Town*, a 1940 selection of FSA photographs with text by Anderson, Rosskam wrote that Stryker's benign influence made the project go: "Stryker lives FSA photography. A former cowboy and professor of economics, he takes no pictures. He has enough on his hands what with budgets, appropriations, and the artistic

Fox chained to an automobile. Moorhead. October 1940. *John Vachon*

temperament of those who take the pictures for him." Other staff members, as well as later studies of the FSA-OWI project, also maintained that Stryker was never a photographer.[20]

The Minnesota material shows that on at least one occasion, however, Stryker did take pictures for the file. When he joined Lee in the field in the spring of 1937, Stryker used a thirty-five-millimeter Leica to take scenes of northern Minnesota, including lumberjacks on the Little Fork River, and of unemployed men in the Gateway district of Minneapolis. Although Stryker may not have aspired to be a photographer, the Minnesota contributions indicate his willingness to try his own hand at the work. Despite his protestations, the pictures offer interesting images. His photograph of Lee's automobile being pulled from the mud illustrates some of the difficulties that the photographers experienced. In all, Stryker took at least forty-eight photographs in Minnesota; two are included in this album.[21]

This new insight into Stryker's experiment with the camera reinforces the understanding that his real genius lay in keeping the organization intact. As head of the Historical Section, he made the assignments for staff members and provided them with detailed instructions to guide them in the field. Throughout the eight years of the project, only four or five full-time photographers were on the staff at any one time; nevertheless, its budget sparked sharp criticism from the press and from Congress. Looking back, Stryker described the development of the FSA-OWI collection as a "bureaucratic miracle." He refuted the notion that the project resulted from his own master plan, giving credit instead to his staff. In his words, the collection was a group effort that grew "like Topsy. . . . We arrived at the right spot at the right time. Some people call it luck. Sure we worked — sure we delivered. But above all *we grew into the project.*"[22]

Although they did not contribute to the Minnesota file, two other people with Minnesota connections worked for the FSA-OWI in the early 1940s. One was Gordon Parks, who attended Mechanic Arts High School in St. Paul. With the support of a Julius Rosenwald fellowship, he worked as an intern in 1942 and 1943; later he became a *Life* photographer, a movie director, and an author. The other was Esther Bubley, a native of Eau Claire, Wisconsin, who studied at the Minneapolis School of Art. She joined the project in 1941 as a lab technician and started working as an OWI photographer the following year.[23]

Our understanding of life during the Great Depression continues to be shaped by the work of Stryker and his photographers. The decade of the 1930s, in the words of Russell Lee, "was a period of real stress in the country, we were in bad shape and all of us knew it. There were people starving, half-starving, God!"[24] Work-worn adults, the men with heads covered by hats and caps and the women wearing cotton print dresses, ill-kept children, eroded farmland, broken-down vehicles, and squalid interiors of houses — these were the subjects of the "cookie cutters," the term applied to the FSA photographs that turned up repeatedly in textbooks and articles depicting the victims of the depression.

Several books issued in the 1980s have presented new material from FSA-OWI files, including many unpublished photographs taken in Ohio, Mississippi, Virginia, Kentucky, Indiana, and Illinois.[25] Standard images of the rural poor with their gaunt faces and thin, tired bodies pass sadly through these collections, yet such people are scarce in the Minnesota images. Physical features like the exteriors of buildings in the cutover region, tents of the blueberry pickers, and slum conditions of the Gateway district reflect the economic hardships that the people endured, but with few exceptions — such as the scenes from the Gateway — the people do not match the surroundings. For example, Lee's photograph of Steve Flanders's daughter drawing water from a shallow well on their northern Minnesota farm surprises the viewer with the girl's stylish attire. The drab interior from the living quarters of a Mexican-American family in the Red River valley provides the background for the happy faces of the family members, frozen in time by Lee's flashbulbs. Vachon's photograph of slum housing in Minneapolis is softened by the presence of the young girl on the curb; the substantial appearance of the buildings contrasts with those shown in slum photographs taken in cities like Cincinnati and Chicago. Lumberjacks, working during the final days of a declining industry, show little regret. In a scene taken by Lee featuring a mock fight, one of the participants is heavily bandaged from a saloon brawl; he seems able to poke fun at himself, however, as well as at the life-style of the lumbering camps and the grim economic realities of the times.

How do we explain the uniqueness of the Minnesota images? Did the photographers who visited the state lack the skill to capture the harshness of the 1930s? Did they record their images after conditions had improved? Or did Minnesotans differ from other Americans caught up in the depression? Elements of truth lie in each of these conjectures. Carter, who took pictures in northern Minnesota in 1936, was less talented than such colleagues as Rothstein, Lange, Evans, Theodor Jung, Carl Mydans, and Ben Shahn, all of whom began contributing to the national file in 1935.[26] But Rothstein, Lee, and Vachon, who also worked in Minnesota, took pictures that have become standard images of the depression years. Rothstein took some of the most poignant pictures in the file, including his photographs of the Dust Bowl and of the distressed coal-mining region of southern Illinois in 1939. When Lee reached Minnesota in 1937 he had just completed several eloquent series in the Midwest featuring tenant farmers, farm auctions, hired hands, and the devastation of the 1937 flood. His sensitivity with the camera and love for detail are evident in all of his pictures. With the exception of the solitary man at the bar in Craigville and the mother and daughter in the saloon at Gemmell, however, his Minnesota pictures have little of the tragic imagery that he found in Iowa, Indiana, and Illinois.

Vachon's assignments in Minnesota came during the later phases of the work of the Historical Section, after the shift in emphasis from poor land and poor people to a celebration of a nation beginning to emerge from the worst years of the depression. Later he was assigned to photograph a nation at war, as were Wolcott and Delano. Throughout his years with the FSA-OWI, Vachon worked with a keen awareness of Stryker's goals for the project, including the continuing need for photographs of people in distress. Despite this awareness, he found few occasions and little need to depict poverty in his home state.

Paul H. Landis, a sociologist who studied the mining towns of Hibbing, Virginia, and Eveleth in the early 1930s, described

Rural school children in Minnesota. September 1939. *John Vachon*

the way of life of the many recent immigrants from Europe — Finns, Slavs, and others who populated the northern region of the state. Writing of St. Louis County, he speculated that the rigorous climate, rocky soil, and "almost unconquerable underbrush make one wonder if any peoples other than sturdy European peasants, who have never known anything but hardships and poverty, would possess the patience necessary to wrest a living from most areas in the County." H. E. Lager, in a memoir entitled *"Happy Depression" on the Iron Range,* echoed this same perception: "Most of the immigrants came here from a destitute and hungry life in the old country." They stayed because nearly all "could see a tangible better life here on the Iron Range." This same understanding could be applied to many of the people living in the sixteen counties in northern Minnesota that were considered to be part of the Great Lakes Cutover region.[27]

Perhaps the stoic determination that pervades the Minnesota collection is explained in part by the ethnic backgrounds of the people in the cutover region and by their adaptation to its harsh climate and soil. Scenes from the rest of the state reflect the relatively better conditions experienced by farmers and farm workers there, as well as the timing of the photographers' visits — mostly after 1937. The absence of faces of defeat reminds us of Stryker's recollection of the FSA-OWI project as a whole: "Probably half of the file contained positive pictures, the kind that give the heart a tug."[28]

This album of Minnesota images includes work by all the FSA-OWI photographers who visited there: Vachon, Lee, Delano, Carter, Rothstein, and Wolcott. They ranged throughout the state between 1936 and 1943, taking pictures in northern Minnesota, the Red River valley, the west-central farming region, and many small communities. This broad geographic coverage of rural Minnesota complements the strong representation of urban photographs, including those taken in Vachon's hometown of St. Paul, neighboring Minneapolis, and the lake port of Duluth. The images are presented in eleven chapters organized primarily by economic activity.

Years after his service with the government project, Vachon wrote an article about the FSA and Stryker. Remembering his long travels west in 1942, Vachon noted that Japan brought the United States into World War II with its sneak attack on Pearl Harbor only a few weeks before he departed. Dispatched to record the war's impact on the domestic scene, he traveled out through Minnesota, the Dakotas, and Montana before swinging back to the East Coast. Vachon recalled: "Our pictures were being used by the Office of War Information, and I was supposed to show that this was a great country. I was finding out it really was. This was a sparsely populated area, still least affected by the war. I didn't know it at the time, but I was having a last look at America as it used to be."[29]

"As it used to be" — Vachon's single phrase captures the significance of the photographs taken by the FSA-OWI photographers, images that picture Minnesotans who are somehow less burdened and perhaps more resolute as they face the challenges of economic depression and international conflict.

NOTES

1. John Vachon to Penny Vachon, January 24, 1942, Vachon Papers, letters and journals in the possession of the Vachon family; John Vachon, "Tribute to a Man, an Era, an Art," *Harper's,* September 1973, p. 98–99. The cameras included a Speed Graphic, a Rolleiflex, and a thirty-five-millimeter Leica. He probably also carried an eight-by-ten-inch Linhof view camera. Robert Vachon (John's brother), interview with author, St. Paul, May 23 and December 31, 1987. See also the articles by John's son, Brian Vachon, "John Vachon: A Remembrance," *American Photographer,* October 1979, p. 34–45, and by his close associate, Thomas B. Morgan, "John Vachon: A Certain Look," *American Heritage,* February 1989, p. 94–109.

2. Edward Steichen, "The FSA Photographers," in *U.S. Camera 1939,* ed. T. J. Maloney (New York: William Morrow and Co., 1938), 44; J. Vachon, "Tribute," 99; Carl Fleischhauer and Beverly W. Brannan, *Documenting America, 1935–1943* (Berkeley: University of California Press, 1988), 335–38 (inclusion of photographs taken under the auspices of the Office of War Information discussed on p. 3). Of the total, 180,000 photographs in the collection were taken by FSA-OWI photographers and the rest were gathered from other sources; 77,000 can be identified as related to Stryker's work. Fleischhauer and Brannan provide the most reliable analysis of the FSA-OWI collection.

3. Here and below, Roy Emerson Stryker and Nancy Wood, *In This Proud Land: America 1935–1943 as Seen in the FSA Photographs* (Greenwich, Conn.: New York Graphic Society, 1973), 7–19. After its original use in a course at Co-

lumbia University, the textbook was published as Rexford Guy Tugwell, Thomas Munro, and Roy E. Stryker, *American Economic Life and the Means of Its Improvement,* 2d ed. (New York: Harcourt, Brace and Co., 1925).

4. Stryker and Wood, *In This Proud Land,* 11; Pete Daniel and Sally Stein, Introduction to *Official Images, New Deal Photography* (Washington, D.C.: Smithsonian Institution Press, 1987), ix (quotation). The latter book, edited by Daniel, Stein, Merry A. Foresta, and Maren Stange, explores the broad subject of government photography during the New Deal.

5. The best study of the FSA is Sidney Baldwin, *Poverty and Politics: The Rise and Decline of the Farm Security Administration* (Chapel Hill: University of North Carolina Press, 1968).

6. Roy E. Stryker to Marion Post [Wolcott], August 11, 1938, Roy E. Stryker Collection, University of Louisville Photographic Archives, Louisville, Ky.; Jack Delano, interview by Richard K. Doud, June 12, 1965, transcript, p. 53, Archives of American Art, Smithsonian Institution, Washington, D.C. Marion Post married Lee Wolcott in 1941. See F. Jack Hurley, *Marion Post Wolcott: A Photographic Journey* (Albuquerque: University of New Mexico Press, 1989).

7. Stryker to Jonathan Daniels (two letters, one personal and one official), September 13, 1943, Stryker Collection. Daniels was administrative assistant to President Roosevelt. From 1943 to 1950 Stryker headed the Standard Oil of New Jersey Photographic Project. Loosely structured around the theme of petroleum, it was the largest photographic documentation project sponsored by a private corporation, amassing some sixty-seven thousand photographs. The collection is housed at the University of Louisville Photographic Archives. See Steven W. Plattner, *Roy Stryker: U.S.A, 1943–1950* (Austin: University of Texas Press, 1983).

8. Hank O'Neal, *A Vision Shared: A Classic Portrait of America and Its People. 1935–1943* (New York: St. Martin's Press, 1976), 20–22.

9. F. Jack Hurley, *Portrait of a Decade: Roy Stryker and the Development of Documentary Photography in the Thirties* (Baton Rouge: Louisiana State University Press, 1972), 76. Carter's brother, John Franklin Carter, was head of the Information Division of the Resettlement Administration and Stryker's supervisor.

10. O'Neal, *A Vision Shared,* 60–63, 75–77. On the Dust Bowl see Donald Worster, *Dust Bowl: The Southern Plains in the 1930s* (New York: Oxford University Press, 1979), and Michael Parfit, "'You Could See It A-Comin': The Dust Bowl," *Smithsonian,* June 1989, p. 44–54, 56–57.

11. The major sources for this information are John Vachon's letters to his mother during 1935 and 1936; his interview with Richard K. Doud, April 28, 1964, a transcript of which is located in the Archives of American Art, Smithsonian Institution; and journals in the Vachon Papers. A good description of the workings of the patronage system in the Resettlement Administration is found in Baldwin, *Poverty and Politics,* 100–102. Vachon's starting salary was $1,080 per year. See also J. Vachon, "Tribute," 96.

12. Vachon to Mother, [Spring] 1936, Vachon Papers; Vachon, interview by Doud, April 28, 1964, p. 12. Vachon did not date his letters. Most of the letters to his wife, Penny, can be dated from the postmark on the envelope.

13. Vachon to Mother, [May] 1937, Vachon Papers.

14. Vachon, interview by Doud, April 28, 1964, p. 15–16.

15. Plattner, *Roy Stryker,* 27; O'Neal, *A Vision Shared,* 267–69.

16. Here and below, O'Neal, *A Vision Shared,* 135–38 (quotation on 135). See also F. Jack Hurley, *Russell Lee, Photographer* (Dobbs Ferry, N.Y.: Morgan and Morgan, 1978).

17. Here and below, O'Neal, *A Vision Shared,* 174–75, 234; Marion Post Wolcott to Stryker, August 2, 1941, Stryker Collection (quotation).

18. Stryker and Wood, *In This Proud Land,* 8.

19. Stryker and Wood, *In This Proud Land,* 11. The original source of the quotation was an interview conducted by Calvin Kytle in 1961; see Kytle's "Roy Stryker: A Tribute," in *Roy Stryker: The Humane Propagandist,* ed. James C. Anderson (Louisville, Ky.: University of Louisville Photographic Archives, 1977), 6.

20. Sherwood Anderson, *Home Town* (New York: Alliance Book Corp., 1940; Mamaroneck, N.Y.: Paul P. Appel, 1975), 145. Plattner quotes Gordon Parks as saying that Stryker "couldn't even load a camera" (Plattner, *Roy Stryker,* 16). Dorothea Lange recalled that Stryker "never dared to leave that desk in Washington. He never went in the field" (interview with Richard K. Doud, May 22, 1964, transcript, p. 20, Archives of American Art). Irene Delano characterized Stryker as a "creative administrator" and noted that he "couldn't take the photographs himself" (Jack and Irene Delano, interview with Richard K. Doud, June 12, 1965, transcript, p. 34, Archives of American Art). Hurley said that Stryker "decided very early to take no photographs himself" (*Portrait of a Decade,* 55).

21. Stryker traveled by train from New York, arriving in Duluth on May 16. He spent ten days in Minnesota with Lee. FSA-OWI Correspondence, reel 7, Stryker Travel, 1937, Library of Congress, Washington, D.C.

22. Stryker to Edna Bennett, August 29, 1962, Stryker Collection.

23. Gordon Parks, *A Choice of Weapons* (1966; reprint, St. Paul: Minnesota Historical Society Press, 1986), 220–51; Parks referred to John Vachon as his "best friend" (interview with author, May 22, 1987). Information on Bubley comes from interview with author, June 9, 1989, and Plattner, *Roy Stryker,* 55.

24. Rob Powell, "An Interview with Russell Lee," *British Journal of Photography,* October 10, 1980, p. 1013.

25. These books include *Ohio: A Photographic Portrait, 1935–1941: Farm Security Administration Photographs,* exhibition organized by Carolyn Kinder Carr (Akron, Ohio: Akron Art Institute, 1980; distributed by Kent State University Press); Patti Carr Black, ed., *Documentary Portrait of Mississippi: The Thirties* (Jackson: University Press of Mississippi, 1982); Brooks Johnson, *Mountaineers to Main Streets: The Old Dominion as Seen through the Farm Security Administration Photographs* (Norfolk, Va.: Chrysler Museum, 1985); Beverly W. Brannan and David Horvath, eds., *A Kentucky Album: Farm Security Administration Photographs, 1935–1943* (Lexington: University Press of Kentucky, 1986); Robert L. Reid, ed., *Back Home Again: Indiana in the Farm Security Administration Photographs, 1935–1943* (Bloomington: Indiana University Press, 1987); Robert L. Reid and Larry A. Viskochil, eds., *Chicago and Downstate: Illinois as Seen by the Farm Security Administration Photographers, 1936–1943* (Urbana: University of Illinois Press, 1989).

26. For information on the FSA work of Jung, Mydans, and Shahn, see O'Neal, *A Vision Shared,* 26–27, 44–47, 115–17.

27. Paul H. Landis, *Three Iron Mining Towns: A Study in Cultural Change* (Ann Arbor, Mich.: Edwards Brothers, 1938), 23–24, 50 (quotation); H. E. Lager, *"Happy Depression" on the Iron Range* (Virginia: Range Printing Co., 1979), 48; Minnesota, Committee on Land Utilization, *Land Utilization in Minnesota: A State Program for the Cutover Lands . . .* (Minneapolis: University of Minnesota Press, 1934), 7, 104.

28. Stryker and Wood, *In This Proud Land,* 14. Reporting on her visit to Otter Tail County in December 1933, journalist Lorena Hickok noted that drought conditions were not so bad in western Minnesota as in the Dakotas. Richard Lowitt and Maurine Beasley, eds., *One Third of a Nation: Lorena Hickok Reports on the Great Depression* (Urbana: University of Illinois Press, 1981), 127.

29. J. Vachon, "Tribute," 99.

Family of an FSA borrower in the cutover farm area. Itasca County. August 1941. *John Vachon*

THE CUTOVER REGION

BY THE TIME Roy Stryker began planning the work of the Historical Section in 1935, the government had identified six regions in rural America as having major problems. These regions included the eastern and western cotton belts, the Appalachian-Ozark area, the short grass / winter wheat and short grass / spring wheat areas, and the Great Lakes Cutover, where loggers had removed the forests and left a vast expanse of unproductive land. A steep decline in farm prices had tumbled gross farm incomes in 1932 to less than half what they had been in 1929. Moreover, the severe drought of the 1930s turned wheat fields from Texas to the Dakotas into a dust bowl, worsening the plight of those who farmed for a living in the Great Plains.[1]

Rural distress in the northern Great Lakes states was not caused by a lack of rainfall, however. Rather, the cutover region suffered from a complex set of conditions that had produced long-standing problems. The cold climate, submarginal agricultural conditions, and demise of the lumbering and mining industries all combined to contribute to the region's malaise. The National Resources Board described this and other rural problem areas as "the slums of the country."

The northernmost counties of Minnesota, Michigan, and Wisconsin, an area of 57 million acres in eighty-six counties, constituted the cutover region — a term that aptly described the stump-dotted, brush-covered landscape. For the half century between 1870 and 1920, this area rang with the sounds of axes and saws when it served as America's timber frontier. In 1890 the Great Lakes forests produced more than one-third of the nation's forest products; by the 1940s, their contribution was less than 5 percent. Following the policy of "cut out and get out," the lumber companies abandoned the area as they depleted the timber, permitting the land to become tax delinquent or selling it to real estate companies. Those who took up farming in the cutover region were often former lumberjacks and miners who had farmed in their spare time. Working against overwhelming odds, they attempted "to scratch out livings between tree stumps, on stony, infertile soil, and on wet, boggy land."[2]

In Minnesota the cutover region was defined in a 1934 state study as including Aitkin, Beltrami, Carlton, Cass, Clearwater, Cook, Crow Wing, Hubbard, Itasca, Kanabec, Koochiching, Lake, Lake of the Woods, Mille Lacs, Pine, and St. Louis counties. Comprising about 40 percent of the total area of the state, the region bore 29,554 farms in 1930. Although these farms constituted 18 percent of the total area, less than 6 percent of the land was in crops. In contrast, 85 percent of the land in the other counties in Minnesota supported farms, most of this acreage under cultivation. The average farm in the cutover region earned $1,107 in 1929, whereas those in other counties in the state earned an average of $2,457. Unlike other rural problem areas of America, this region did not attract large numbers of tenant farmers. Difficult agricultural conditions restricted farm operations to one-family units, resulting in a lower percentage of tenant farming than in the rest of Minnesota.[3]

Noting that past misuse explained the economic malaise of the cutover region, Governor Floyd B. Olson wrote in 1934:

Forest land that should never have been stripped of its timber, land that should never have been put under cultivation, swamps that should never have been drained, isolated settlements that should never have been permitted in places far removed from roads, schools, and other social services, unwise and premature development that should never have been undertaken — all have contributed to create the problem of idle land and stranded communities.[4]

Local, state, and federal governments eventually combined efforts in an attempt to solve the problems of the region.

Responding to requests from federal extension service employees in the area, Stryker sent Russell Lee to the cutover region in the spring of 1937. N. S. Boardman, regional director, wrote that the extension service needed "good pictures of land conditions" in an area "eloquent on the story of timber exploitation and forest fires."[5] A new project of Harcourt, Brace and Company also called for images, "a book of photographs illustrated by a poem," in the words of its author, Archibald MacLeish. Stryker wrote to Lee that the book's theme would be the "story of the driftwood left by the high waters, the floods, the expansion and swift onrush in [the] development of America in the 19th and 20th centuries." He wanted pictures of those "left behind after the empire builders had taken the forests, the ore, and the topsoil."[6]

Specific objectives for the photo project in the cutover region included "the people, the way they live, their isolation," "the look of the country," interiors of homes and stores, iron mining, and lumbering. In encouraging Lee to visit the tough lumbering town of Hurley, Wisconsin, Stryker wrote: "These pictures will be for the private files of Americans, of which you are a stockholder." He also noted, "We will be about the first people to have done a very good study of the cut-over people so you may consider yourself a pioneer."[7]

Making one of his rare appearances outside Washington, D.C., Stryker actually joined Lee in the field. Stryker, who wanted "a chance to see something of the difficulties in the field," observed Lee's technique in getting people to cooperate with the photographer.[8] During this trip he took the photograph of Lee's automobile being pulled from the mud, as well as images of the logjam on the Little Fork River and the Gateway district in Minneapolis. Pictures taken by John Vachon in 1939 and 1941 in northern Minnesota complete the selections in this chapter. The rest of the book includes other photographs of the people of the cutover region and of economic activities there — lumbering, mining, and farming.[9]

NOTES

1. Here and below, P. G. Beck and M. C. Forster, *Six Rural Problem Areas: Relief — Resources — and Rehabilitation: An Analysis of the Human and Material Resources in Six Rural Areas with High Relief Rates,* Federal Emergency Relief Administration, Division of Research, Statistics and Finance, Research Section, Research Monograph 1 (Washington, D.C., 1935), 9–24; D. Jerome Tweton, "The Business of Agriculture," in *Minnesota in a Century of Change: The State and Its People Since 1900,* ed. Clifford E. Clark, Jr. (St. Paul: Minnesota Historical Society Press, 1989), 263; U.S., National Resources Board, *A Report on National Planning and Public Works in Relation to Natural Resources and Including Land Use and Water Resources with Findings and Recommendations* (Washington, D.C.: Government Printing Office, 1934), 156–57, 175–97 (quotation on 175).

2. Walter A. Rowlands, "The Great Lakes Cutover Region," in *Regionalism in America,* ed. Merrill Jensen (Madison: University of Wisconsin Press, 1951), 331–32, 344 (quotation); Orlando W. Miller, *The Frontier in Alaska and the Matanuska Colony* (New Haven, Conn.: Yale University Press, 1975), 48 (quotation).

3. Committee on Land Utilization, *Land Utilization in Minnesota,* 7, 13. The statistics for farm income are based on a fourteen-county study reported in H. F. Hollands, "Income and Standard of Living," in *A Program for Land Use in Northern Minnesota* by Oscar B. Jesness, Reynolds I. Nowell, and Associates (Minneapolis: University of Minnesota Press, 1935), 84–89. Tenancy rates reached a peak of 34 percent in Minnesota in 1935; Lowry Nelson, *The Minnesota Community: Country and Town in Transition* (Minneapolis: University of Minnesota Press, 1960), 10–11.

4. Committee on Land Utilization, *Land Utilization in Minnesota,* vi.

5. R. I. Nowell to Dr. W. W. Alexander, May 13, 1937, N. S. Boardman to Dr. W. W. Alexander, August 27, 1937, both in Record Group 96, Region II, Field Correspondence, box 2, National Archives, Washington, D.C.

6. Archibald MacLeish, *Land of the Free* (New York: Harcourt, Brace and Co., 1938; reprint, New York: Da Capo Press, 1977), 89 (this book included one Minnesota photograph, by Russell Lee); Stryker to Lee, April 16, 1937, Stryker Collection.

7. References to this series appear in the Stryker-Lee correspondence, January 19 and 20 and April 3–27, 1937, Stryker Collection.

8. Stryker to Lee, January 19, 1937, Stryker Collection. Stryker traveled by train from New York to Duluth via Chicago, arriving on May 16. He left Minneapolis on May 26 for Madison, Wisconsin. FSA-OWI Office Files, Library of Congress.

9. Skala's Cafe is the restaurant in Tower where Lee photographed the bill of fare. The photograph taken in a beer parlor in Gemmell depicts Big Alice's Tavern, whose proprietor was Alice Simmons (Harold Curb, Gemmell resident, interview with author, May 27, 1989).

Filling a can with water from a shallow well on a farm in the cutover area. Northome (vicinity). September 1937. *Russell Lee*

Opposite: Home of Steve Flanders. Northome (vicinity). September 1937. *Russell Lee*

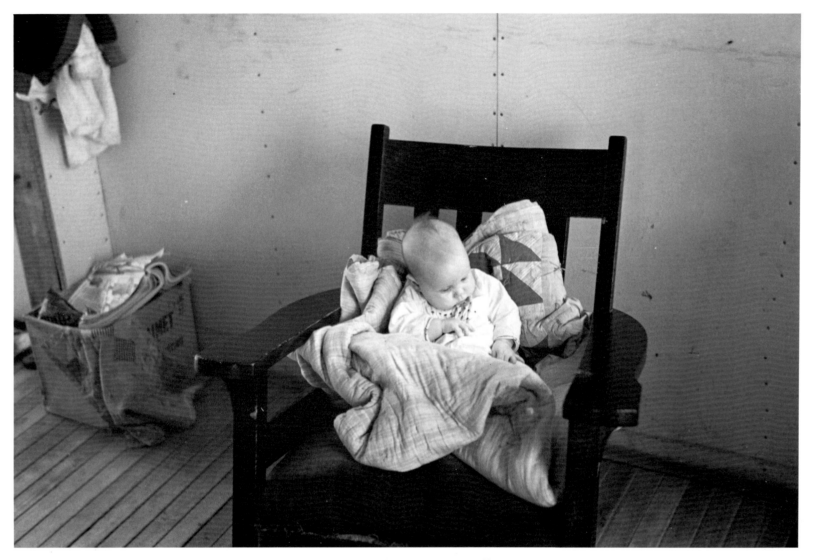

Baby of family in a cutover area. Northome (vicinity). September 1937. *Russell Lee*

Residents of Northome. [September 1937. *Russell Lee*]

Boardinghouse. Little Fork. September 1937. *Russell Lee*

Farmer in the cutover area, taking a pinch of snuff. Little Fork (vicinity). September 1937. *Russell Lee*

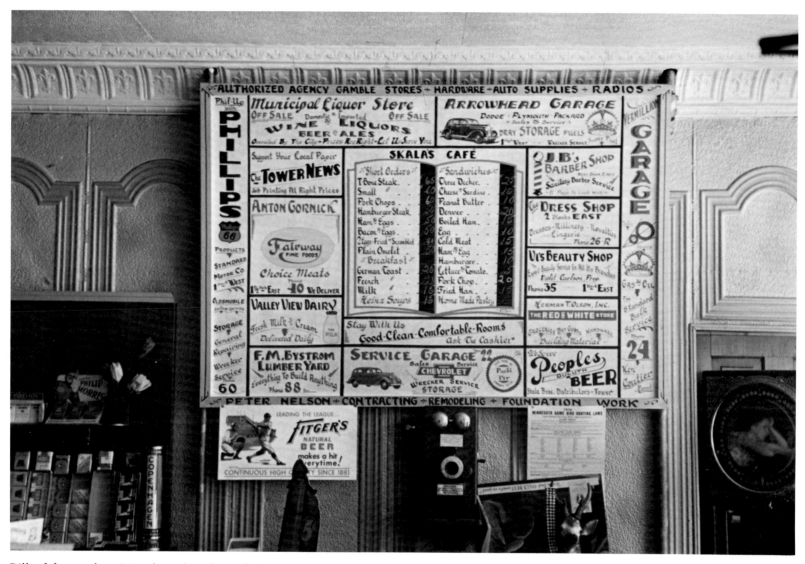

Bill of fare, advertising board and goods in restaurant. Tower. August 1937. *Russell Lee*

OPPOSITE: An old house in a formerly prosperous lumbering town. Tower. August 1937. *Russell Lee*

House and automobile belonging to a farmer in the cutover area. Lake of the Woods County. September 1939. *John Vachon*

Farm Security Administration photographer being pulled out of the mud by a tractor. Little Fork (vicinity). 1937. *Roy Stryker*

An old resident. Winton. August 1937. *Russell Lee*

Former bank, now a saloon.
Mizpah. August 1937.
Russell Lee

Farmers at the S. W. Sparlin sale. Orth. August 1937. *Russell Lee*

Farm woman at an auction sale waiting for her husband. Tenstrike (vicinity). September 1939. *John Vachon*

Old resident in the corner of a beer parlor of this formerly prosperous lumbering center. Note the sign and the battery-operated radio. Gemmell. August 1937. *Russell Lee*

Resident reading a newspaper in a general store. Funkley. August 1937. *Russell Lee*

County FSA supervisor visiting the family of an FSA rehabilitation borrower. Lake of the Woods County.
September 1939. *John Vachon*

FSA PROJECTS

BETWEEN 1933 and 1935, several New Deal agencies — the Federal Emergency Relief Administration (FERA), the Rural Policy Section of the Agricultural Adjustment Administration, and the Division of Subsistence Homesteads of the Department of the Interior — experimented with programs designed to relieve chronic rural poverty. Congress merged these programs in 1935 and placed them under a new agency, the Resettlement Administration, to give better direction to the government's efforts in land use planning, rural relief, and resettlement. Two years later Congress replaced the Resettlement Administration with the Farm Security Administration.[1]

Northern Minnesota was the site of one of the nation's earliest resettlement projects. The Beltrami Island Settler Relocation Project included one and a half million acres in the cutover forest area of Beltrami, Koochiching, Lake of the Woods, and Roseau counties. Poor soil, cold winters, a short growing season with an average of 112 frost-free days, and bad drainage all worked against those who turned to farming following the depletion of the forests. In 1934 about 480 settlers lived in this vast region, where basic public services such as roads, relief, and schools (the area was unable to support a high school) were costly to maintain. Medical care was almost nonexistent, and there was only one church. Because tax delinquency was high and the average annual family income was low — less than three hundred dollars from all sources — taxpayers throughout the state subsidized the few who lived in this sparsely settled area.[2]

The Beltrami Island project, which was initiated by the Min-nesota Department of Conservation and the Minnesota Rural Rehabilitation Corporation, received approval from the FERA in December 1934. The project combined rehabilitation of the forests, including the development of wildlife refuges and recreational opportunities, with the retirement of submarginal land and the relocation of needy families. The government bought the land on which these families lived and made loans to enable them to purchase land in more desirable sites of their choosing within the four-county area. They could get additional low-cost loans to buy seed, equipment, and supplies. Much of the credit for the success of the Beltrami Island project was attributed to local control and to project manager Archie D. Wilson. In less than four years, 95 percent of the families moved voluntarily to more desirable locations. Two new state forests, Beltrami Island and Pine Island, were established by the state and administered by the Department of Conservation. The Beltrami Island project led to state zoning laws that restricted settlement on lands designated as submarginal.[3]

In a similar attempt to solve the problems of the tax-delinquent, scattered population living on the submarginal land of the Great Lakes Cutover, the Works Progress Administration (WPA) — a federal program usually associated with urban relief efforts — conducted the Matanuska Colony project. In 1935 the project resettled 201 families from the cutover regions of Minnesota, Wisconsin, and Michigan in the Matanuska Valley of Alaska. Although the project was never administered nor photographed by employees of the Resettlement Administration or its successor, the FSA, critics often cited it as an example of wasteful government planning in rural resettlement. The high costs of the Alaskan project and the boldness of the plan attracted national attention by the media, including the press and movie newsreels. This publicity helped make other Americans aware of the hardships encountered by those who lived in the northern Great Lakes region.[4]

Roy Stryker sent Paul Carter to northern Minnesota to cover Beltrami Island in 1936. Noting the difficulty of capturing the problems of stranded settlers on film, Stryker wrote: "Isolated schoolhouses and roads serving a limited number of people are very expensive items for the taxpayers of any county to maintain. This offers one of the best arguments for Resettlement, particularly so when one or two families living in an isolated region necessitate the maintenance of roads and schoolhouses. We need pictures to illustrate this situation."[5] Carter's photographs of the Yankoski family, including the makeshift cabin used to transport the children to school during the winter, provided dramatic evidence for the FSA files. Three years later, John Vachon visited the cutover region. On his eight-day trip through northern Wisconsin and Minnesota he took pictures at the Northern Minnesota Pioneer Home, which housed people displaced by the Beltrami Island project. Located in Spooner, a twin village to Baudette on the south bank of the Rainy River, it was described by Vachon as "a home for eight old men, all over 70, former lumberjacks and bachelor farmers." He found this the most interesting story of his trip. At Williams, also in northern Lake of the Woods County, Vachon photographed the Northern Farmers' Cooperative Exchange. Working through county extension agents across the nation, this cooperative seed-marketing association sold more than 3 million pounds of alfalfa and clover seed in 1939.[6]

Three of the ninety-nine subsistence homestead projects completed under the New Deal were located in Minnesota: Austin Acres, Duluth Homesteads, and Albert Lea Homesteads. The Historical Section photographers visited only Austin, where Carter took some rather prosaic images of the buildings and of people gardening and canning. In these projects, the govern-ment built homes on relatively large plots of land. Homesteaders were expected to hold industrial jobs and to supplement their incomes by planting vegetable gardens. The initiative for the Austin project came from business and financial leaders in the community. Jay C. Hormel, president of the meat-packing company that employed about three thousand of the city's population of eighteen thousand, headed the local campaign. On December 15, 1933, the secretary of the interior authorized the local corporation, Austin Subsistence Homesteads, Inc., to purchase 216 acres within a mile of the city at an average price of forty-eight dollars per acre. The corporation developed plans to build forty-four houses, and it received more than 350 applications. Income requirements were well above the poverty level. Moreover, only residents of Austin could apply, and 70 percent of the homesteaders had to be Hormel employees. When the federal government asserted control over all such programs in 1934, it retained these same guidelines.[7]

The houses, standing on three- to five-acre plots south of Austin, were completed in September 1935. Three years later the FSA sold the property to a nonprofit corporation composed of the homesteaders. Individuals leased their homes under contracts with an average purchase price of $1,450 per unit, to be paid over forty years at $18 per month. Austin Acres, with its large lots and curving roads, remained an attractive residential area in the 1980s. A resident described the homesteads as quiet, peaceful, and a "wonderful place to raise children"; several of the original families continued to live there and were responding to an annexation plan that was initiated by the city of Austin in 1985.[8]

A similar pattern prevailed at Duluth where the local Chamber of Commerce took the lead, also in the fall of 1933. Development moved slowly, with Duluth Homesteads — located west of the city near Hermantown — taking shape under the auspices of the Resettlement Administration. The eighty-four units were not fully occupied until March 1938. Perhaps the slow development of this project explains the lack of photographs of it. Since extensive files existed for similar projects in other states, perhaps the FSA saw little need for pictures of this site. Also, by the time the project was completed, the impetus for further projects had diminished as the federal government consolidated its many programs of relief, recovery, and reform.[9]

Planned communities like Austin Acres and Duluth Homesteads received a disproportionate amount of attention from both media critics and political opponents of the New Deal, who attacked these "radical" attempts by the government to assist the rural poor. Those who opposed this form of government intervention cited excessive costs and unnecessary frills, such as the community building at Austin Acres. When Congress created the Farm Security Administration in 1937, federal farm policy turned away from resettlement projects. The remaining photographs in this chapter, taken by Vachon, portray FSA borrowers, their families, and county extension agents engaged in a variety of rural activities.[10] These efforts to rehabilitate by offering loans for seed, fertilizer, livestock, and equipment, together with expert advice, precipitated much less controversy than had the subsistence housing projects.

NOTES

1. James S. Olson, ed., *Historical Dictionary of the New Deal: From Inauguration to Preparation for War* (Westport, Conn.: Greenwood Press, 1985), 9–13, 165–67, 176–77, 419–20, 477–78.

2. Two separate projects, Beltrami Island and Pine Island in adjoining Koochiching County, became popularly known as the Beltrami Island project; here and below, R. W. Murchie and C. R. Wasson, *Beltrami Island, Minn. Resettlement Project,* University of Minnesota, Agricultural Experiment Station Bulletin 334 ([Minneapolis], 1937), 5, 7, 15–22, 24; Farm Security Administration, "Report on Beltrami Island Farms (Minnesota)," June 25, 1940, Record Group 96, box 24, National Archives, p. 1–2.

3. A. D. Wilson, "Settler Relocation: A Description of the Minnesota Plan," *Journal of Land and Public Utility Economics* 14 (November 1938): 402–16. On Wilson's key role in making the project a success, see Carl Henry Stoltenberg, "Progress in Rural Zoning in Northeastern Minnesota" (Ph.D. diss., University of Minnesota, 1952), 117, and "Rural Zoning in Minnesota: An Appraisal," *Land Economics* 30 (May 1954): 154–55.

4. The best study of the Matanuska project is Miller, *Frontier in Alaska.*

5. Stryker to Arthur Rothstein, May 23, 1936, Stryker Collection.

6. FSA, "Report on Beltrami Island Farms," 6–7; news release on Williams Seed Festival, October 7, 1939, Record Group 96, box 736, National Archives; Vachon to Stryker, September 18, 1939, Stryker Collection.

7. Paul K. Conkin, *Tomorrow a New World: The New Deal Community Program* (Ithaca, N.Y.: Cornell University Press, 1959), 332–37 (the population figures are for 1939); here and below, Russell Lord and Paul H. Johnstone, eds., *A Place on Earth: A Critical Appraisal of Subsistence Homesteads,* U.S. Department of Agriculture, Bureau of Agricultural Economics (Washington, D.C., 1942), 59–63. The records for the three Minnesota subsistence homestead projects have been withdrawn from Record Group 96 in the National Archives and are apparently lost.

8. *Progressive Austin, 1935–36* (Austin: Junior Chamber of Commerce, [1935]), 28; William Milbrath, interview with author, Austin Acres, September 12, 1987 (quotation).

9. The best study of Duluth Homesteads, based on the Duluth Homesteads Papers at the University of Minnesota, Duluth, is Timothy J. Garvey, "The Duluth Homesteads: A Successful Experiment in Community Housing," *Minnesota History* 46 (Spring 1978): 2–16. The Albert Lea project, which was classified as an industrial site and built under the authority of the FERA, was limited to fourteen houses. U.S., Farm Security Administration, *Hearings before the Select Committee of the House Committee on Agriculture to Investigate the Activities of the Farm Security Administration,* pt. 3 (Washington, D.C.: Government Printing Office, 1944), 1069.

10. On the role of county extension agents in the 1930s, see Roland H. Abraham, *Helping People Help Themselves: Agricultural Extension in Minnesota, 1879–1979* ([St. Paul]: Minnesota Extension Service, University of Minnesota, 1986), 121–42. The Resettlement Administration was planning eight additional sites in 1936; a review of the project records indicates that only two scattered farm projects, one near Litchfield called Central Minnesota Farms and the other at Thief River Falls, were initiated. Senate, Resettlement Administration Program, *Letter from the Administrator of the Resettlement Administration Transmitting in Response to Senate Resolution No. 295 . . . ,* 74th Cong., 2d sess., 1936, S. Doc. 213 (Serial 10007), p. 38, 42. The Central Minnesota project, which was based on long-term loans, received laudatory testimony in the 1943 House investigation of the FSA. U.S., Farm Security Administration, *Hearings before the Select Committee,* pt. 1 (Washington, D.C.: Government Printing Office, 1943), 399–404.

Grading seed which a farmer has brought into the office of the Border King cooperative seed exchange, to determine the purity and quality of the seed before a price is set on it. This cooperative was financed by an FSA loan which has been repaid.
Williams. September 1939. *John Vachon*

The Yankoski family standing by the front door of their log house. Beltrami Island reforestation project of the Minnesota state forest service. July 1936. *Paul Carter*

The Bendix schoolhouse, in an unorganized territory, forty-five miles from the county seat, five miles from the Yankoski home. Beltrami Island reforestation project. July 1936. *Paul Carter*

This cabin was mounted on a sleigh last winter to transport four children to and from school. A stove was kept inside to protect them from the severe cold. The children only missed one day of school the entire winter. Beltrami Island reforestation project. July 1936. *Paul Carter*

Farmer in the cutover area, moving his house to a new land. The government bought the land on which he formerly lived to take it out of farming. Lake of the Woods County. September 1939. *Paul Carter*

Father and daughter who have been resettled on this farm. Beltrami Island reforestation project. July 1936. *Paul Carter*

A subsistence homestead project of the U.S. Resettlement Administration. Woman hanging out clothes. Austin. August 1936. *Paul Carter*

A subsistence homestead project of the U.S. Resettlement Administration. Homesteader canning vegetables in her new kitchen. Austin. August 1936. *Paul Carter*

Card game in the Northern Minnesota Pioneer Home which was established by the government to care for the former squatters and lumberjacks who were displaced from their homes in the Beltrami Island area. Spooner. September 1939. *John Vachon*

Finnish lumberjack, now ninety years old, a resident of the Northern Minnesota Pioneer Home. Spooner.
September 1939. *John Vachon*

Resident of the Northern Minnesota Pioneer Home. Spooner. September 1939. *John Vachon*

Home supervisor examining the garden of an FSA borrower. Mille Lacs County. July 1941. *John Vachon*

Wife of an FSA borrower coming from storage cellar with jars of canned fruit on their cutover farm land. Itasca County. July 1941. *John Vachon*

Wife of an FSA borrower in the storage cellar on their farm in the cutover area. Itasca County. July 1941. *John Vachon*

One of the bulls in the FSA-financed bull cooperative. This bull is transported to farms of rehabilitation clients for service. Itasca County. September 1939. *John Vachon*

Tenant purchase borrower loading hay into the barn. Freeborn County. August 1941. *John Vachon*

Ladies who live in the rooming house. St. Paul. September 1939. *John Vachon*

THE TWIN CITIES

THE MINNESOTA FILE contains an unusually strong representation of urban scenes. Probably no other state — with the exception of Illinois, where Russell Lee, John Vachon, and Jack Delano did extensive work on Chicago and the black belt — can display as many photographs taken of city life. This resulted, in part, from the strong impression that Roy Stryker formed of Minneapolis when he visited the city with Lee in 1937. The major explanation, however, is found in Vachon's visits home, which he used as opportunities to photograph the Twin Cities.[1]

The Twin Cities of Minneapolis and St. Paul emerged in the late nineteenth century as the center of the economic and cultural life of the Upper Midwest. St. Paul's early success can be attributed to its strategic location at the terminus of steam navigation on the upper Mississippi River. Following its merger with a third rival, St. Anthony, in 1872, Minneapolis developed as the city beside the waterfall — the Falls of St. Anthony. Sawmilling, flour milling, and railroading, its principal enterprises, spurred its development as a trade and service center. Minneapolis established national leadership in sawmilling. The "City of Lakes" also led in flour milling until 1930, when Buffalo, New York, surpassed it in flour production for the first time. The construction of a national railroad system, including two transcontinentals that linked the Twin Cities with the Pacific Northwest, established Minneapolis-St. Paul as one of the regional centers of an increasingly interdependent urban-industrial society.[2]

The FSA photographs of the Twin Cities feature a variety of buildings, people, and activities. In 1930 Minneapolis was the dominant twin, with a population of 464,356; St. Paul, the capital city, had a population of 271,606. The metropolitan area — both cities and their suburbs — included more than one-third of Minnesota's population. Vachon made his initial contributions to the Minnesota file in 1939 on a specific assignment to cover the Twin Cities as well as small towns. In a letter to Marion Post Wolcott, Stryker described the set of photographs taken by Vachon in Minnesota as "swell things." She replied, "I'm glad John did so well — I was sure he would. He's damn good."[3]

Two years earlier, when Lee and Stryker visited Minneapolis, they concentrated their work in the Gateway district, an area that Vachon also photographed in 1939. Located at Bridge Square, this urban skid row was dominated by flophouses, saloons, liquor stores, pawn shops, and employment agencies. As early as 1910, more than one hundred flophouses and hotels and at least that many saloons and liquor stores were found in the Gateway, once the hub of business life in Minneapolis and the site of the original city hall in the years before 1900. Two well-traveled avenues, Nicollet and Hennepin, fanned out from the square and crossed another, Washington; the Mississippi River bounded the square on the northeast. Described by writer Meridel Le Sueur as the "hiring center for the northwest," during the 1930s the Gateway offered the largest concentration of unskilled, unemployed laborers in the Upper Midwest. Lumberjacks, miners, and farm workers found refuge in the flophouses, where they paid from twenty-five to fifty cents per night for a bunk. The novelist Sinclair Lewis, a native of Sauk

Centre, called the Gateway "as ugly a section as you could find in any American city." The scenes depicted by Stryker, Lee, and Vachon were familiar to visitors to downtown Minneapolis until urban renewal came in the late 1950s.[4]

One feature of life in the Gateway was religious enterprise. Both Lee and Stryker photographed the bearded man outside the Minneapolis Holiness Mission Church at 114 Hennepin Avenue. Other photographs in Minneapolis include the 1939 Vachon picture of the River-Lake Gospel Tabernacle, which was headed by successful radio evangelist Luke Rader. The prophetic sermon title reads, "Will America Go to War?" A photograph of symbols and exhortations, crudely painted by hand, presents another statement of religious fundamentalism. Jack Delano took the photograph of the Reverend Emil Swenson, pastor of Bethlehem Lutheran Church and president of the Minnesota Conference of the Augustana Lutheran Church, as part of his series on Swedish Americans in 1942.[5]

The Mississippi River and the early downtown skylines dominate the photographs of Minneapolis and St. Paul. The most compelling images for the photographers, however, particularly for Vachon, were the grain elevators and flour mills. Elevators provided exciting opportunities to take pictures that would display texture and space through light and shadows. Vachon's image of the structure with tar patches illustrates this interplay. He took more than sixty pictures of grain elevators during his September 1939 visit, a number comparable to the number of such structures in Minneapolis.[6]

Lee extended his coverage of Mexican-American sugar beet workers by photographing the first annual Independence Day celebration in St. Paul on September 15–16, 1937. Reflecting the blend of cultures, the celebration recognized two important events—the beginning of the Mexican revolt from Spain on September 16, 1810, and the 150th anniversary of the U.S. Constitution. Lee's photograph of a children's recitation during the ceremony appears in this chapter, and one showing a dance at Our Lady of Guadalupe mission church appears in the chapter entitled "Leisure Time."[7]

Vachon took his photograph of St. Paul with the houses in the foreground from the High Bridge, looking northeast to downtown. It depicts the housing area known as the Upper Levee flats, an Italian neighborhood isolated from the city by bluffs and railroad tracks. In the 1930s, fifty years after the original families settled the area, 80 percent of the one hundred families living there were Italian. Although most homes in the area lacked baths and inside toilets, almost all had electricity and water. Persons of Mexican-American and Italian heritage made up small minorities in both Minneapolis and St. Paul; Swedes and Norwegians dominated Minneapolis, and St. Paul was a city of Germans and Irish.[8]

Lee and Stryker centered their attention on the Gateway in Minneapolis, tying this to their coverage of lumbering and mining in the cutover region. Arthur Rothstein, Wolcott, and Vachon all found the grain elevators, primarily in Minneapolis, worthy subjects for their cameras. As a result, fewer pictures of St. Paul went into the collection, limiting the selection for this book. Rothstein's picture of a St. Paul elevator appears in the chapter entitled "Roads, Rails, and Waterways." In a personal image, the scene of the Vachon home at 2171 Lincoln Avenue shows the photographer's younger brother, Robert Vachon, picking up the morning newspaper.

NOTES

1. In a letter to his mother in June 1937, John Vachon wrote: "Stryker is back from Minnesota. He spent some time in Minneapolis [and] . . . wants to get pictures of the town." Vachon Papers. FSA photographs from urban Illinois are found in Reid and Viskochil, eds., *Chicago and Downstate*.

2. Good sources for an account of this development include Lucile M. Kane, *The Falls of St. Anthony: The Waterfall That Built Minneapolis* (1966; reprint, St. Paul: Minnesota Historical Society Press, 1987), 41, 77, 115, 173; Robert H. Wiebe, *The Search for Order: 1877–1920* (New York: Hill and Wang, 1967); John R. Borchert, *America's Northern Heartland* (Minneapolis: University of Minnesota Press, 1987).

3. John R. Borchert, "The Network of Urban Centers," in *Minnesota in a Century of Change,* ed. Clark, 57; U.S., *Census,* 1930, vol. 1, *Population,* p. 10; Stryker to Marion Post [Wolcott], October 17, 1939, Post to Stryker, October 25, 1939, Stryker Collection.

4. Here and below, Lucile M. Kane and Alan Ominsky, *Twin Cities: A Pictorial History of Saint Paul and Minneapolis* (St. Paul: Minnesota Historical Society Press, 1983), 32, 62–65, 213; Le Sueur, *North Star Country* (New York: Duell, Sloan and Pearce, 1948), 283; David L. Rosheim, *The Other Minneapolis: or, The Rise and Fall of the Gateway, the Old Minneapolis Skidrow* (Maquoketa, Iowa: Andromeda Press, 1978), 55–57, 132–33, 153, 185–87. The Lewis paraphrase is from William H. Kelty, review of *Can Our Cities Survive?* by José Luis Sert, *Minneapolis Tribune,* March 21, 1943, society, club and women's section, p. 11.

5. Lutheran Church in America, Minnesota Synod, *Minutes of the Seventh Annual Convention* ([Minnesota]: The Synod, [1968]), 85.

6. Kane and Ominsky, *Twin Cities,* 207; Robert Vachon, interview with author, May 23, 1987; Robert M. Frame III, "Grain Storage and the Development of the Elevator," in *A Guide to the Industrial Archeology of the Twin Cities,* ed. Nicholas Westbrook (St. Paul and Minneapolis: Society for Industrial Archeology, 1983), 63.

7. Lee to Ed Locke, September 15, 1937, Stryker Collection; St. Paul, International Institute, Inc., and the Neighborhood House, comps., "A Study of the Mexican Community in St. Paul: Released September 1946" (St. Paul: The Institute, [1946]), typewritten manuscript, photocopy in Minnesota Historical Society (MHS), p. 11.

8. Hildegard Binder Johnson, "The Germans," 169, 178, Carlton C. Qualey and Jon A. Gjerde, "The Norwegians," 231–33, Ann Regan, "The Irish," 140, John G. Rice, "The Swedes," 261, and Rudolph J. Vecoli, "The Italians," 453, all in *They Chose Minnesota: A Survey of the State's Ethnic Groups,* ed. June Drenning Holmquist (St. Paul: Minnesota Historical Society Press, 1981), 453; Alice L. Sickels, "The Upper Levee Neighborhood: A Study of an Isolated Neighborhood of about One Hundred Italian Families in St. Paul, Minnesota . . ." (Master's thesis, University of Minnesota, 1938), 64.

Unemployed men in the Gateway district. Minneapolis. September 1939. *John Vachon*

A street scene. Minneapolis. [May or June] 1937. *Roy Stryker*

Employment agency in Gateway district. Minneapolis. September 1939. *John Vachon*

Pawnshop in the Gateway district.
Minneapolis. September 1939.
John Vachon

Goodwill store
and mission church.
Minneapolis.
May 1937.
Russell Lee

Gospel tabernacle. Minneapolis. September 1939. *John Vachon*

Symbols and exhortations. Minneapolis. September 1939. *John Vachon*

Dr. Emil Swenson is the pastor of [a Lutheran] church at 22d and Fremont [avenues north], Minneapolis. . . . [He] was born in Kansas but his parents came from the province of Värmland, Sweden. Minneapolis. March 1942. *Jack Delano*

Flour mills along the river. Minneapolis. September 1939. *John Vachon*

OPPOSITE: Grain elevator with tar patches. Minneapolis. September 1939. *John Vachon*

Tattered billboard. Minneapolis. September 1939. *John Vachon*

OPPOSITE: Flour mill. Minneapolis. August 1941. *Marion Post Wolcott*

Brewery. Minneapolis. September 1939. *John Vachon*

Slum housing. Minneapolis. September 1939. *John Vachon*

Recitation by Mexican girls at the Independence Day celebration. St. Paul. September 1937. *Russell Lee*

Dog pound. St. Paul. September 1939. *John Vachon*

St. Paul. September 1939. *John Vachon*

Morning paper. St. Paul.
October 1940. *John Vachon*

Packing flour in the Pillsbury mills.
Minneapolis. September 1939.
John Vachon

WORKERS IN TOWNS AND CITIES

☐ AS THE FSA PROJECT evolved, Roy Stryker and his photographers recognized the need to document the relationship between rural and urban America. Stryker developed "shooting scripts" that called for images depicting small towns and large cities, as well as the countryside. The photographers paid special attention to work-related activities, taking pictures that would show the manufacturing process from the raw material in the field to the finished product on the grocer's shelf. In addition to the major industries of lumber and iron mining, the Minnesota file includes photographs of corn and other grains, sugar beets, flour, and dairy products.

John Vachon's familiarity with the files gave him certain advantages, foremost of these the education he received from studying the work of Walker Evans, Dorothea Lange, Russell Lee, and others. His knowledge of the collection enabled him to recognize gaps in the coverage. As his fieldwork increased, Vachon saw an opportunity to add needed material by combining his photographic assignments with a visit to his St. Paul home. He told Stryker about his father, Harry, a paper supply salesman whose territory included western Minnesota. Vachon indicated that he could travel out from St. Paul with his father and photograph his customers, hoping to produce "a complete set of pictures on the midwestern small town, including all types of respectable citizens." This dream was realized in 1939 when he photographed scenes of people at work, such as newspaper employees at Brown's Valley and Litchfield, a pharmacist at Graceville, and a banker at Park Rapids. Vachon also photo-graphed work activities in Minneapolis and the cutover region during this trip.[1]

Two years later, when Vachon returned to the Midwest, Stryker encouraged him to photograph various aspects of food processing. In particular, Stryker asked for "a series of pictures of the slaughtering of hogs and cattle." Vachon tried to photograph such scenes at the Union Stock Yards in Chicago but was refused permission. Stryker replied that he "was not surprised about the slaughtering pix. As you remember Time/Life printed gore and details of [a] prize 4-H steer slaughter. Well, the packing companies caught hell for this and so did Life."[2]

From Chicago Vachon traveled to Minnesota, where he took more urban photographs. In a letter to his wife, Penny, he speculated that the Hormel plant in Austin might offer a good possibility for pictures of slaughtering. On July 22 he wrote letters to Penny and to Stryker, boasting of his achievement. Vachon arrived at Hormel at 7:00 A.M. and, through a misunderstanding that he helped foster, was given what he called "carte blanche." He reported that he stood "in six inches of purple black blood firing flash bulbs at dismemberment." At noon the plant photographer accompanying him caught "hell" from his boss. During the afternoon and the next morning Vachon worked under tight restrictions, while the Hormel photographer sought without success to retrieve the negatives from that first morning session. "I am now a vegetarian," Vachon wrote, the result of his coverage of the "gory story of slaughtering." The two selections here make it clear why the meat packers resisted such pictures.[3]

Another Vachon photograph from his 1941 trip shows butter packing at the Land O' Lakes Creameries plant in Minneapolis. This enterprise was the nation's largest producers' cooperative; Minnesota, with its strong Scandinavian tradition, led the United States in both producers' and consumers' cooperatives. Started as a project of dairy farmers who organized a statewide association in 1921, Land O' Lakes became the leading supplier of butter in the nation. Vachon enjoyed his visit to the factory where the butter was packaged and shipped. At the Minneapolis plant he was accompanied by a "Scandinavian boy guide, dairy major from U of M [University of Minnesota]." Following World War I, Americans consumed increasing amounts of milk and milk products. The growth of Land O' Lakes was based on this trend; its success also reflected the dramatic changes in rural life during the twentieth century. The interdependence that is characteristic of urban, industrial society is a major theme in these photographs of people making a living.[4]

NOTES

1. Vachon to Mother, three letters from fall 1938 to fall 1939, Vachon Papers; Vachon to Stryker, September 1939, Stryker Collection. The banker is John Flynn, president of the State Bank of Park Rapids (J. D. Smythe to author, June 12, 1989). The mother and daughter in the Right Spot Tavern in Gemmell are Mrs. Joe King and Ernestine (Harold Curb, interview with author, May 27, 1989).

2. Stryker to Vachon, June 27, July 5, 1941, Stryker Collection.

3. Vachon to Penny, July 22, 1941, Vachon Papers; Vachon to Stryker, July 1941, Stryker Collection.

4. Kenneth D. Ruble, *Men to Remember: How 100,000 Neighbors Made History* (N.p.: Privately published, 1947), 3–18, 246; Vachon to Penny, July 13, 1941, Vachon Papers. On cooperatives, see a 1936 description by Minnesota Congressman Ernest Lundeen in *Congressional Record,* 74th Cong., 2d sess., 1936, 80, pt. 6: 6739–62. He noted that Minnesota had more cooperatives, both producer and consumer, than any other state.

Makeup man for the Litchfield Independent helping editor of the high school paper. Litchfield. September 1939. *John Vachon*

The editor of the Valley News getting a news item by telephone. Brown's Valley. September 1939. *John Vachon*

Newsstand in the Gateway district. Minneapolis. September 1939. *John Vachon*

Picketing. Minneapolis. September 1939. *John Vachon*

Slitting throats of cattle at the Hormel meat-packing plant. Austin. July 1941. *John Vachon*

Processing hog innards at the Hormel meat-packing plant. Austin. July 1941. *John Vachon*

Packing butter cut into squares at the Land O' Lakes plant for use in restaurants. Minneapolis. July 1941. *John Vachon*

Unloading milk cans at cooperative creamery which has received a loan from the Farm Security Administration. Coleraine. September 1939. *John Vachon*

President of the bank. Park Rapids.
September 1939. *John Vachon*

Mother and daughter in a saloon-restaurant. The mother is the proprietor. Gemmell. August 1937. *Russell Lee*

Lumberjacks at a logging camp. Effie (vicinity). September 1937. *Russell Lee*

LUMBERJACKS

WITH THEIR CAMERAS, the FSA photographers caught the last days of Minnesota's lumber industry. The Great Lakes forest regions of Minnesota, Wisconsin, and Michigan were exhausted. Forests within Minnesota were "no longer able to meet even the local needs for lumber," according to a 1934 state study. The Minnesota timber frontier, which opened up in 1837 in the delta between the St. Croix and Mississippi rivers, gradually moved north with the seemingly inexhaustible pine stands. Great Lakes lumbering produced 35 percent of the total lumber cut in the United States in 1890, declining from this peak to 4 percent by 1939.[1] Writer Walter Havighurst described the cutting of the northern forests as "the great enterprise" of the region, "dwarfing all others in its drama and riches." Lamenting the demise of the industry, Governor Elmer A. Benson said in 1937 that lumbering had been "the very backbone of the economic life of the State." The magnificent white and red pines, some two hundred feet tall with trunks five feet in diameter, fell as Minnesota, the last of the white-pine states, lost its abundant forests. Recalling his visits to the Great Lakes Cutover region some twenty-seven years later, Russell Lee said, "It was beyond comprehension what they did up there and there was no effort at conservation or anything like that!"[2]

Roy Stryker sent Lee to the area in the spring of 1937. His visit coincided with Minnesota's "last great log drive," the International Lumber Company's cutting of the last major stand of white and red pine from the Nett Lake Indian Reservation. Hundreds of lumberjacks worked to send logs containing an estimated 13 million feet of lumber down the Nett and Little Fork rivers to the Rainy River. The lumber landed at the storage and hoist booms at Loman on the Canadian border, about one hundred miles away. From Loman the logs were shipped by rail to sawmills at International Falls. Reported to be the "biggest operation of its kind in recent years," the drive was expected to last about thirty days. Both Lee and Stryker, who joined him to experience the work of his photographers at first hand, took photographs of one phase of the drive, the breaking of a logjam near the town of Little Fork. They saw the lumberjacks using the peavey — a combination cant hook and pike point — to roll the logs back into the river in one of the most dangerous operations of the entire logging enterprise.[3]

Folktale and ballad often present logging as a romantic occupation; in reality, the job entailed dangerous, back-breaking labor in isolated camp settings. The lumberjacks worked long days in cold temperatures through the winter months. Lee captured both the rigors of the work and the social life of the lumberjacks when he visited a lumber camp near Effie in August and September 1937. One photograph features the camp cook calling the workers to dinner in the evening; another shows the dinner table where the loggers ate in silence, a tradition of the industry. The cook used his five-foot-long tin horn to rouse the men at 4:00 A.M. for the day's work. Although lumber companies strictly prohibited alcohol, Lee found two men sharing a bottle in the bunkhouse. Each of his pictures of lumberjacks reflects his careful attention to detail.[4]

Lee also took pictures of northern Minnesota logging communities, virtually all in decline; some had become ghost towns. In their heyday, these places had been noted for their lawless atmosphere. Playing with this theme, Stryker wrote facetiously to Lee describing International Falls as "one of the toughest towns on the border. It is a meeting place of lumbermen, Indian traders, trappers, smugglers, immigration refugee smugglers, and so on. They used to kill a man every morning before breakfast and one just before supper, just for amusement." Lee described Gemmell as a town of five hundred people that once had forty-seven lumber camps employing more than seven thousand men; trains of logs went "thru every 15 minutes." Several of Lee's photographs from Gemmell appear in other chapters.[5]

At nearby Craigville, Lee provided evidence of the important role the saloon played in the social life of the lumberjack. Visiting on "payday in the lumber town," he captured several poignant interior scenes on film. The men dissipated hard-earned wages on gambling, whiskey, and women in the saloons, brothels, and "bath houses" of these towns. The aftermath is revealed in humorous fashion in the image of the individual "beaten up and 'rolled' in a saloon . . . on Saturday nite" sharing the scene with two buddies posed in mock battle. Stryker wrote, "Your saloon pictures are superb."[6] His conclusion — "The set on life in the lumber camp is tops" — aptly describes Lee's visual record of the lumber industry in Minnesota.[7]

NOTES

1. Committee on Land Utilization, *Land Utilization in Minnesota,* 14 (quotation); R. V. Reynolds and Albert H. Pierson, *Lumber Cut of the United States, 1870–1920: Declining Production and High Prices as Related to Forest Exhaustion,* U.S. Department of Agriculture, Bulletin 1119 (Washington, D.C.: Government Printing Office, 1923), 30–35; Marx Swanholm, *Lumbering in the Last of the White-Pine States,* Minnesota Historic Sites Pamphlet Series 17 (St. Paul: Minnesota Historical Society, 1978), 8; Miller, *Frontier in Alaska,* 51.

2. Havighurst, *Upper Mississippi: A Wilderness Saga* (New York: Farrar and Rinehart, 1937), 153; Benson, "Conservation and the Lumberjack," *American Forests* 43 (August 1937): 381; Lee, interview by Richard Doud, June 2, 1964, Archives of American Art.

3. Agnes M. Larson described an earlier "last log drive" in 1934 on Rainy Lake in her definitive study, *History of the White Pine Industry in Minnesota* (Minneapolis: University of Minnesota Press, 1949), 401; Stryker to Lee, April 21, 27, 1937, Stryker Collection; *Daily Journal* (International Falls), April 5, p. 19 (quotation), p. 24, May 4, 1937 (quotation). A photograph from the Minnesota and Ontario Paper Company depicting the Little Fork River filled with logs was included in Grace Lee Nute's *Rainy River Country: A Brief History of the Region Bordering Minnesota and Ontario* (St. Paul: Minnesota Historical Society, 1950), following p. 58. Nute called this the "last great drive" (p. 123). A film entitled "The Last Log Drive on the Little Fork" (1976), based on footage taken at the time by an amateur photographer, is available from the Education Department of MHS.

4. Harold Curb has identified the camp cook as Henry Leseman (interview with author, May 27, 1989). A photograph of Leseman also appears in Lorraine Albrecht and Dolly Thomas, *Northome – Mizpah – Gemmell: Minnesota History, 1903–1977* (N.p.: Northome Centennial Book Committee, 1977), 88.

5. Stryker to Lee, April 23, 1937, Stryker Collection; description on back of negative LC-USF 34-30521A, FSA-OWI Collection.

6. Lee to Ed Locke, September 15, 1937, FSA-OWI Correspondence; caption for photograph LC-USF 33-11352-M1, FSA-OWI Collection; Stryker to Lee, October 30, 1937, Stryker Collection. For a lively account of life in a lumber town, see Anne Anderson (Peggy) Mattice, interview by John Esse, July 8, 1975, transcript, Audio-Visual Library, MHS. Mattice operated a Craigville saloon in the 1940s that was frequented by lumberjacks and prostitutes.

7. Stryker to Lee, October 21, 1937, Stryker Collection. A feature that used some of Lee's photographs, "Life in the Lumber Camps," appeared in *Building America: Illustrated Studies of National Problems,* vol. 4, no. 6 (1939): 12–13, a publication of the National Education Association. See also "Minnesota Logging Camp, September 1937: A Photographic Series by Russell Lee," selected and introduced by Carl Fleischhauer, Beverly W. Brannan, and Claudine Weatherford, *Folklife Annual 1986* (Washington, D.C.: Library of Congress, 1987), 108–31.

Lumberjack turning handspring.
Little Fork (vicinity).
June 1937. *Russell Lee*

Going to work at a lumber camp. Effie (vicinity). September 1937. *Russell Lee*

OPPOSITE: Lumberjacks using peaveys to remove logs from the banks of the Little Fork River. Little Fork (vicinity). May 1937. *Russell Lee*

Loaders pushing logs into place while loading a rail car. Effie (vicinity). September 1937. *Russell Lee*

A logging camp. A lumberjack at a camp, with a stake which he has shaped with a broadaxe. Effie (vicinity). September 1937. *Russell Lee*

A logging camp. The camp cook blowing the dinner horn. Effie (vicinity). September 1937. *Russell Lee*

Lumberjacks at dinner at a logging camp. Effie (vicinity). September 1937. *Russell Lee*

Drying silverware. Effie (vicinity). September 1937. *Russell Lee*

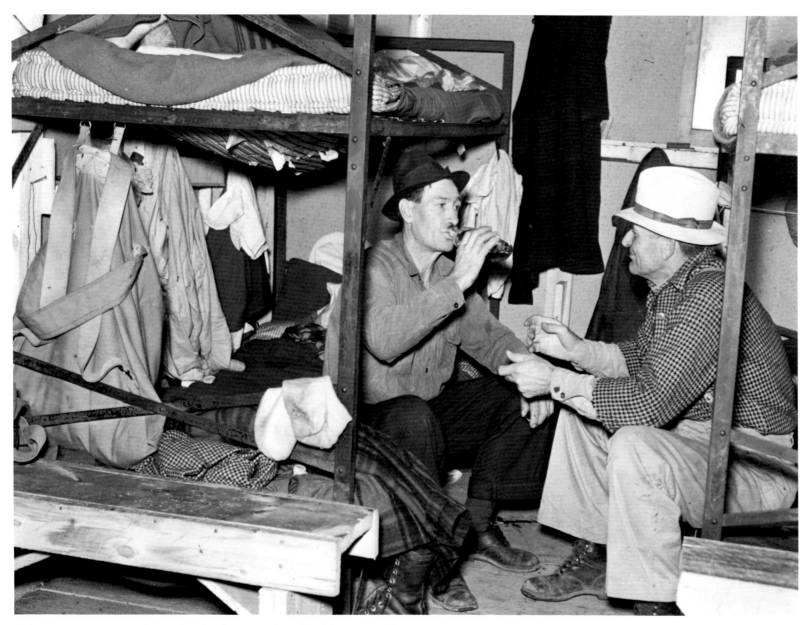

A logging camp. Lumberjacks drinking in their bunkhouse. Effie (vicinity). September 1937. *Russell Lee*

A lumberjack washing his feet.
Effie (vicinity). September 1937.
Russell Lee

Lumberjacks in the hotel lobby at [Dusmar] Hotel. Many of the men that rise early spend a few hours here reading and talking before going to work. Little Fork. September 1937. *Russell Lee*

Main Street. Craigville. September 1937. *Russell Lee*

Steam baths are very popular among the lumberjacks. Craigville (vicinity). August 1937. *Russell Lee*

Saturday night in a saloon. Craigville. September 1937. *Russell Lee*

A man at the bar on Saturday night. Craigville. September 1937. *Russell Lee*

William Besson, an iron ore prospector, examining the geological survey maps in his cabin. Winton (vicinity).
August 1937. *Russell Lee*

THE IRON RANGES

BESIDES AGRICULTURE, Minnesota's economic history centered on three major industries — lumbering, milling, and mining. During the Great Depression, lumbering continued the decline that had started at the turn of the century, while grain merchants and millers shared in the agricultural slump that American farmers had experienced for almost a decade before the stock market crash of 1929. Although the steel industry was hard hit by the depression and mining was severely curtailed, Minnesota continued to provide the raw material, producing two-thirds of the nation's iron ore. During the 1930s total annual production from the three iron ranges — the Mesabi, Vermilion, and Cuyuna — averaged 40 million tons of ore. With the coming of World War II, activity stepped up. Shipments from the open-pit mines of the Mesabi exceeded 70 million tons in the single year of 1942.[1]

Commercial development began in 1884 when the Minnesota Iron Company completed a railroad line from the new town of Tower on the Vermilion Range to the port of Two Harbors on Lake Superior. In 1890, Leonidas Merritt and his six brothers discovered ore beds on the Mesabi Range, where the iron ore was a red earth easily mined at the surface. They started open-pit mining, and the rail lines that were soon built provided the means to carry the ore to docks at Duluth and its sister city of Superior, Wisconsin. In the next several years, such major entrepreneurs as John D. Rockefeller, Andrew Carnegie, J. P. Morgan, and James J. Hill established control of the Mesabi. America's richest deposit of iron ore became part of the vast holdings of the nation's first billion-dollar corporation when U.S. Steel was organized in 1901.

The other side of the enterprise was presented in Meridel Le Sueur's evocative study of the Upper Midwest, where she wrote: "Human history is work history." She described the development of the iron ranges in this way:

> The great crust of the Algonquian rock that lay, a ring of iron, under the Great Lakes in the ranges, Mesabi the Giant, the Vermilion, Cayuna [sic], Gogebic, Menominee, Marquette, had to be shoveled, lifted, hauled to their harbors, loaded into boats, shoveled into the holds, unloaded at the other end of the journey; by hand, shoulder muscle, the small of the back, the loins, the leg muscles — working ten, twelve, fourteen hours a day.[2]

Because they also record work history, the photographs of the mining industry taken by Russell Lee and John Vachon complement Le Sueur's words. No mineowners appear in these images; instead, they feature the men and the machines that produced the iron ore.

Lee photographed one of the last pioneers of the industry when he visited an old mining prospector, William S. Besson. Like the Merritt brothers, Besson had been both a timber cruiser and an iron hunter. He was eighty-one years old and had lived in the area of Winton for about fifty years. Besson told the photographer that the "process of mine prospecting as pictured is essentially the same as years ago." Lee noted that Besson worked two to four hours a day and that he classified himself as a recluse, which he defined as "someone who lives alone but who improves himself and his mind—a hermit simply lives by himself."[3]

Winton, at the northeast corner of the Vermilion Range, had been founded in the early 1890s as a lumbering town. Some 1,800 men worked in the lumbering industry of this area until 1914, when mill operations ceased. As a mining community, Winton was most active during the years from 1910 until 1925; the mine that employed 500 men was closed that year. In 1937 Lee reported that "most of the population is now supported by iron mines nearby, by the tourist trade (it is the jumping off place for famous canoeing and fishing country) and trapping." Overall he found a "bad situation among the iron miners on the iron range," who worked only a few months each year.[4]

In contrast to Lee's nostalgic photos of Besson, the unpainted store building, and the abandoned miners' houses at Babbitt, Vachon's images, taken in 1941, show active miners employed at the world's largest open-pit mine, the Hull-Rust-Mahoning at Hibbing, and at the Danube mine near Bovey. The expansion of the mines exploiting the huge Mesabi ore deposit forced the largest of the iron range communities, Hibbing, to move one mile south of its original location in 1919. The original site—called North Hibbing—rapidly vanished in the 1930s. With a population of fifteen thousand, Hibbing enjoyed the benefits of a state tax policy that rewarded the local communities. Some of the nation's most opulent educational facilities, including a $4 million high school, served the city.[5]

When letters of authorization were late in arriving from Roy Stryker in the summer of 1941, Vachon resorted to deception to get permission to photograph the mines and loading docks. He confessed in a letter to his wife that he had lied and said he was doing defense committee work. Unlike his colleague Jack Delano, who was known for his meticulous camera work, Vachon "took pictures fast in case I was caught." Vachon's concerns about government security reflected the growing tensions of a world plunged once again into war. Japanese incursions into China in 1937 and Germany's invasion of Poland in 1939 had brought on World War II. In the summer of 1941, the United States prepared for war as it provided aid to Great Britain. In contrast to the early 1930s, when unemployment on the iron ranges was estimated to be as high as 70 percent, the 1941 photographs of the miners present an industry gearing up for full production.[6] When the FSA Historical Section was merged into the Office of War Information in 1942, Vachon's striking photographs of mining became part of the collection available to the new agency.

NOTES

1. Here and below, Theodore C. Blegen, *Minnesota: A History of the State,* 2d ed. (Minneapolis: University of Minnesota Press, 1975), 363–74. See also David A. Walker, *Iron Frontier: The Discovery and Early Development of Minnesota's Three Ranges* (St. Paul: Minnesota Historical Society Press, 1979).

2. Le Sueur, *North Star Country,* 18, 227–28.

3. Notes on back of No. 1140, box 24, FSA-OWI Correspondence; [Ely's] Roaring Stoney Days Celebration, Historical Committee, *A Souvenir Booklet . . . in Commemoration of Ely 70th Birthday, 1888–1958* ([Ely]: Privately published, 1958), 62.

4. Benson, "Conservation and the Lumberjack," 381; notes on back of No. 1142, box 24, FSA-OWI Correspondence; Lee to Stryker, [August] 1937, Stryker Collection. The store in Tower is Konst Martilla, Confectionery (Dana Miller, Iron Range Research Center, Chisholm, interview with author, May 28, 1989).

5. Landis's *Three Iron Mining Towns* discusses the adaptations that the communities of Hibbing, Eveleth, and Virginia made as their nonrenewable wealth was depleted. See also Works Progress Administration, *The WPA Guide to Minnesota* (1938; reprint, St. Paul: Minnesota Historical Society Press, 1985), 322–24.

6. Vachon to Penny, August 13, 1941, Vachon Papers; Blegen, *Minnesota,* 524.

Store in an iron range town.
[Tower.] August 1937.
Russell Lee

Abandoned miners' houses at Babbitt. This mine has not operated since about 1925, but still is kept in repair with the remote prospect of opening at some future time. Babbitt. September 1937. *Russell Lee*

Member of the blasting crew at the Danube iron mine. Bovey (vicinity). August 1941. *John Vachon*

Blasting crew and their foreman at the [Danube] iron mine. Bovey (vicinity). August 1941. *John Vachon*

One end of the Hull-Rust-Mahoning pit, the largest open-pit iron mine in the world. The pit is two and one-half miles long, three-fourths mile wide, and about four hundred feet deep. Hibbing (vicinity). August 1941. *John Vachon*

111

The Hull-Rust-Mahoning mine,
the largest open-pit iron mine
in the world. Hibbing (vicinity).
August 1941. [*John Vachon*]

Moving railroad tracks in the Mahoning iron pit. Hibbing. August 1941. *John Vachon*

Electric shovel at the Mahoning iron mine loading ore into railroad cars at the rate of eight cubic yards per shovelful. Hibbing. August 1941. *John Vachon*

Iron ore from the Minnesota range in the Great Northern railroad yards. Superior, Wisconsin. August 1941. *John Vachon*

Main Street. Hibbing. August 1941. *John Vachon*

Pat McRaith and one of his nieces milking. He is milking seventeen cows this winter on 160-acre farm. Meeker County. February 1942. *John Vachon*

A FARM FAMILY

IN 1937 Roy Stryker said to John Vachon: "When you do filing, why don't you *look* at the pictures. . . . And if you ever decide you want to take pictures, don't say, 'I'm going to take pictures like Russell Lee,' but say, 'I'm going to learn to take pictures.' Say, '*I've* got some ideas.'" Vachon's initial experiments with cameras gave rise to ideas that led to several series, including his coverage of work in small towns in Minnesota in 1939.[1] Another brought him back to Minnesota to make a significant addition to the photographic files on his home state.

Vachon's idea was to visit the farm in Meeker County where his younger brother, Robert (Bob), worked each summer. "I could get pictures of a type I'd be unable to get on farms where I was absolutely a stranger." He wanted to take "home life pictures — intimate things, making pies, cleaning the house, sitting around the radio after dinner," as well as exterior scenes of the "farmer digging in to prepare for winter, putting machines away, erecting snow fences." John Vachon proposed this idea to Stryker while in Minnesota in the fall of 1939, at the same time that he was promoted to junior photographer at an annual salary of $1,800.[2]

A few years earlier, Ann Vachon had learned through a neighbor of an opportunity for her fourteen-year-old son to gain summer employment. She made arrangements for Bob to work on the farm of Jeremiah (Jerry) and Frances (Fanny) McRaith near Hutchinson in the summer of 1936. The young man worked for his board and room. He so enjoyed his experiences that he "talked incessantly" about farming when he returned

home that fall. Bob spent the next four summers as a "hired man" in Meeker County. He loved farming and was proud of the steady increases in his salary, which equaled that of a regular hired man — thirty dollars per month — in the summer of 1940.[3]

The McRaiths, an Irish Catholic family with ten children, owned and operated the "home place" and adjoining farms in the southeastern corner of Meeker County. Jerry and Fanny gave their children a choice of receiving forty acres of land or a college education. Three sons and a daughter, Arthur L., Michael J., Patrick J., and Mary (Mrs. Joseph McCormick), chose farming. Virtually all of the property had been swampy bottomland when Jerry purchased it in 1892, and he drained the swamps over the years to make them suitable for cultivation. In 1936 Pat and Mike managed the main farm of 180 acres, Art farmed 100 acres to the east, and the McCormicks had a smaller farm to the north. Two years later Mike married and bought a 75-acre farm in Wright County near Montrose, some thirty-five miles from the McRaith farms.[4]

Bob's letters home to his mother capture the feelings of a city boy adapting to rural life. He described his immediate boss, Pat, as "a swell fellow to work for." Each day began early when Jerry, then seventy-six years old, called Pat "at five sharp, but Pat doesn't get up until five-thirty and neither do I." This "same old grind up at five-thirty and to bed about nine" left Bob with little time for reading, one of his favorite pastimes. He was elated on the day when Pat gave him the keys to the 1936 Chevrolet. "Today I was sitting in the car," Bob wrote. "Pat got into the back seat and told me to drive it, he told me what to do and I drove it around about four miles right over to another farm and I kept stopping and starting all the way." Bob advised his parents to save their money as he was doing "because we have to buy a car."[5]

The automobile was one manifestation of the sweeping technological changes taking place in American agriculture. The McRaith farms, like others throughout the Midwest, were being transformed from self-sufficient operations with occasional annual profits to ones that increasingly stressed commercial production. Besides the automobile, new machinery — especially the tractor — came into use virtually overnight. In Meeker County this development coincided with an epidemic of equine encephalitis (sleeping sickness) that killed hundreds of horses. Farmers purchased rubber-tired, all-purpose tractors that they found "could do nearly every task as well, if not better, than the horse," reported a contemporary account. By 1942 nine out of ten farmers in the countryside around the nearby village of Dassel reportedly owned tractors. The McRaiths purchased their first, an A Model John Deere, in 1937; that same summer the Rural Electrification Administration authorized construction of power lines, and electricity came to the farm. The McRaiths were typical of farmers in southern and central Minnesota. They raised a herd of dairy cows, a flock of chickens, and several hogs on the home place, using corn and oats as the principal feed crops and growing varying amounts of other grains, including wheat and barley, as cash crops. Like many other Minnesota farmers, the McRaiths got through the worst years of the depression with the help of New Deal agricultural programs. As a result Jerry and Fanny were fiercely loyal to President Roosevelt.[6]

In two visits to the McRaith farms in October 1940 and February 1942, John Vachon created a photographic essay that was similar to the stories featured in the new popular magazines *Life* and *Look*. He described Stryker's reaction when he proposed photographing a family that he could approach through his brother: "He went for it big . . . and keeps reminding me

of it."[7] The images have a special quality of openness because of Bob's acceptance by the McRaiths. This relationship, combined with John Vachon's sensitivity with the camera, enabled the photographer to capture such activities as making beds, mending harnesses, and milking cows, as well as the personalities of Jerry, Fanny, Pat, Mike, the McRaith grandchildren, and Bob Vachon. John's love of music and night life, whether in a Chicago jazz club or a country store, is reflected in his photographs of a Friday night dance at the Lake Stella Store. The pictures feature such scenes as two musicians, couples dancing, and an exuberant Pat McRaith. The next morning John Vachon reported himself up at 5:30 A.M. photographing "milking operations." After viewing the finished prints, he wrote: "Tell Bob they make an excellent set of pictures . . . [and include] a beautiful shot of Pat and Elaine milking."[8] Taken almost fifty years ago, the photographs still fit John Vachon's description as an "excellent set of pictures."

Bob Vachon did not go into farming, becoming instead a manufacturer's representative in the plumbing supply business. In 1989 he lived in St. Paul in the neighborhood where he and John grew up. One McRaith granddaughter, Elaine McCormick, was married to Frank Ray and lived in St. Cloud. Her sister, Mary Catherine McCormick Leath, lived in Seattle, Washington. Jerry McRaith, the boy photographed as he watched his father, Mike, mend harnesses, became a successful grocer in Waverly. Mike McRaith moved from his farm near Montrose during World War II to another farm near Winsted in McLeod County, where he continued to farm. His brother, Pat, was seventy-seven years old and still lived on the home place, farming with his sons as his father had done before him. John McRaith, a grandson of Jerry and Fanny, was the freckle-faced boy beside the 1940 license plate in the photograph on the cover of this book. A priest, he served as director of the National Catholic Rural Life Conference before becoming bishop of the Owensboro Diocese in Kentucky.[9]

NOTES

1. B. Vachon, "John Vachon," 36.

2. Two letters, John Vachon to Mother, [September and October 1939], Vachon Papers; Stryker to Vachon, September 20, 1939, Stryker Papers. Vachon recalled that he did not receive the title of junior photographer until November 1940 (Vachon, "Tribute to a Man," 98). Hurley wrote that Vachon was officially classified as a photographer in 1941 (*Portrait of a Decade,* 156).

3. Vachon to Penny, December 12, 1936, Vachon Papers; Robert Vachon, interview with author, May 23, 1987. John wrote to his wife that Bob "has been raised to 30 bucks a week and is pretty seemingly happy about the whole thing" (August 18, 1941, Vachon Papers).

4. John McRaith, December 8, 1987, and Michael McRaith, January 1, 1988, interviews with author.

5. John McRaith, interview with author, December 8, 1987; series of undated letters in 1936, Robert Vachon to Mother, Vachon Papers.

6. Doris A. Pearson, "Dassel: Past and Present: A Survey of Recent Changes in an Agricultural Community" (Term paper, University of Minnesota, 1942), copy in Reference Library, MHS, 1–9, 17–21 (quotation on 4). The A Model had steel wheels, indicating that Pat and Mike were skeptical of the new rubber tires.

7. John Vachon to Mother, October 1939, Vachon Papers. The photographs of Mike and his family were taken near Montrose in Wright County, as indicated in the corrected captions (John McRaith, interview with author, December 8, 1987).

8. Vachon to Penny, February 18, 1942; Vachon to Mother, [March or April 1942], Vachon Papers.

9. In the 1980s the McRaiths continued to plow around a stone monument located a quarter mile from the farmhouse. It marked the site where Little Crow, leader of the Dakota party in the conflict of 1862, was killed while picking raspberries by two farmers, Nathan Lamson and his son Chauncey, on July 3, 1863. The monument was erected by the state in 1929. Gary Clayton Anderson, *Little Crow: Spokesman for the Sioux* (St. Paul: Minnesota Historical Society Press, 1986), 7–8, 178; Kenneth Carley, *The Sioux Uprising of 1862,* 2d ed. (St. Paul: Minnesota Historical Society, 1976), 86; Robert Vachon, May 23, 1987, John McRaith, December 8, 1987, Michael McRaith, January 1, 1988, and Patrick McRaith, May 29, 1989, interviews with author.

Mr. and Mrs. McRaith, who live on a farm. Meeker County. October 1940. *John Vachon*

Farmer tuning in the radio.
Meeker County. October 1940.
John Vachon

Elaine McCormick, one of the McRaith
grandchildren, making the beds
in the morning before the
school bus comes. Meeker County.
February 1942. *John Vachon*

Old Mr. and Mrs. McRaith, Pat, the hired man, and one of the grandchildren at lunch. Meeker County. February 1942. *John Vachon*

Mike McRaith repairing harness;
his son Jerry is watching. [Wright County.]
February 1942. *John Vachon*

Farm girl putting wood into the kitchen stove.
Meeker County. October 1940. *John Vachon*

Pat McRaith's hired man pouring milk into cans.
Meeker County. February 1942. *John Vachon*

House and buildings of the young owner of a 120-acre farm. [Wright County.] October 1940. *John Vachon*

Farmers' dance in crossroads store. Meeker County. February 1942. *John Vachon*

Music supplied by two Meeker County farmers for dance at crossroads store. Meeker County. February 1942. *John Vachon*

Farmers' dance in crossroads store. Meeker County. February 1942. *John Vachon*

An Indian blueberry picker. Little Fork (vicinity). September 1937. *Russell Lee*

WORKERS IN THE COUNTRYSIDE

DURING THE 1930s agriculture continued to be Minnesota's most important basic industry. In 1938 the WPA publication *Minnesota: A State Guide* reported that the state's 203,000 farms encompassed almost 33 million acres, or two-thirds of its area; the guide classified more than half of the population as rural.[1] John Vachon, Russell Lee, and their colleagues documented a state that was dominated by farming, an enterprise that employed more people and produced more revenue than any other sector of the economy. Within that sector, a transformation was under way as mechanization, heavy use of chemicals to fertilize the soil, and federal agricultural policies combined to change farming from a labor-intensive to a capital-intensive industry. This revolution helped bring about a very different America from the one portrayed by the FSA photographers.

In the late nineteenth century Minnesota had been known as the breadbasket of the nation, primarily because of its specialization in wheat. By the 1930s, this one-crop dominance had given way to a diverse agricultural economy. Corn, oats, barley, and rye were now important cash and feed crops. The "prosperity quintuplets"—cows, cattle, hogs, sheep, and chickens—produced three-fourths of the farm income of Minnesota. Corn and other grains provided the food that fattened the cattle and hogs for market and kept the cows and hens producing milk and eggs. With annual production totaling 150 million bushels, corn became the state's leading crop.

Although the grain and livestock complex extended throughout Minnesota, this pattern of commercial farming was concentrated in the south. The rolling countryside of the southeast, with its rich and productive soil, lent itself to diversified farming. During the drought years, rainfall was higher in this region than in those bordering the Dakotas. As a result, southeastern counties experienced the lowest relief rates in the state: 3.5 percent in Goodhue, 4 in Wabasha, 5 in Jackson, Mower, Nicollet, and Scott, and 6 in Faribault and Houston. Relief levels in Minnesota counties to the west and north ranged from 12 to 60 percent.[2]

Meridel Le Sueur captured the despair of the drought years as she recounted a journey through western Minnesota and the Dakotas:

> The dust now becomes so thick, the driver must drive very slowly. It grinds against the windshield. We drive as if going to a funeral; the corpse is the very earth. The houses are closed and stand in the haze hardly visible, unpainted, like the hollow pupa when life has gone. But you know that everywhere in those barricaded houses are eyes drawn back to the burning windows, looking out at next winter's food slowly burning.
>
> The whole countryside bears not only its present famine but its coming hunger. No vegetables now and worst of all, no milk. It is monstrous with this double doom! Every house is alike in suffering; hundreds of thousands of such houses from state to state. . . .
>
> When I shut my eyes, the flesh burns the eyeballs and all I can see is the sign visible now of starvation and famine,

ribs, the bones showing through the skin, rising over the horizon.[3]

The severe decline in farm prices and the resulting militant farm protest movement, as seen in the Farmers' Holiday Association of 1932, took place before the creation of the Historical Section in 1935. Drought only worsened the situation, and as late as 1937 conditions were still uneven. Lee noted that "the whole region of the Dakotas, Montana and northern Minnesota have suffered from short crops. The Red River Valley had the best — about half a crop."[4] Except for Lee's photographs, most of the following scenes of agriculture in Minnesota were taken in the later years of the New Deal when the situation was improving. The only agricultural discontent expressed in this series is the chalkboard message at the grain elevator in Rice County: "See the Bankers for credit — We Owe them Plenty."

Roy Stryker sent Arthur Rothstein to Iowa and Minnesota in the fall of 1939 to photograph "the story of corn." This series included Rothstein's pictures of the farm manager, his wife, and a hired man at the successful dairy farm of Henry A. Brandtjen, located between Rosemount and Farmington in Dakota County. Three years later an area to the east comprising 11,500 acres became part of the Gopher Ordnance Works, as the war turned Rosemount into a boom community.[5] On this visit Rothstein also photographed an onion harvest in Rice County. Marion Post Wolcott took two classic images — one of a grain elevator at Sauk Centre and the other of fields of corn and wheat near Fergus Falls — as she traveled west to Montana in 1941.

The FSA photographers also visited the Red River valley and the cutover region. Lee took pictures of the two major crops grown in this fertile area bordering the Dakotas: potatoes, which had joined wheat as an important cash crop, and sugar beets, introduced into central Minnesota in the early 1900s and the Red River valley during the 1920s. Processing plants were built in East Grand Forks and consolidated in 1934 as the American Crystal Sugar Company.[6] The industry was very labor intensive, with migrant workers coming from Mexico and Texas to harvest the crop each September. They pulled the beets from the ground and removed the leafy tops with broad knives. Writing to Dorothea Lange, whose photographs of migrant workers in California were among the most memorable images of the depression years, Stryker commented that some of Lee's photographs "look as if he might just as well have been in California as in the Lake States — same primitive houses, bad camps, and so on." Although growers originally brought the Mexican Americans north as seasonal laborers, during the 1930s many settled in the Twin Cities, especially in the West Side neighborhood of St. Paul. A 1936 survey indicated that 86 percent of Minnesota's Mexican-American population of four thousand were classified as beet workers.[7]

Agricultural scenes from the cutover region centered on the town of Little Fork, an area familiar to Lee because of his work there on the lumber industry. Although he missed the wild rice harvest, Lee took more than fifty photographs of Ojibway people from the Red Lake Indian Reservation. These images depict another harvesting activity, blueberry picking in Koochiching County, which the Indians did both for sale and home consumption.

Alfalfa, one of the most important crops of the cutover region and a perennial used for forage, was also grown for seed and marketed through such cooperatives as the Northern Farmers' Cooperative Exchange at Williams. Technically, the machinery used to remove the seeds was a huller, a modified version of a threshing machine, although Lee used the term "threshing alfalfa seed" in his caption. The image makes clear the vital role of machinery in this dirty, arduous task.[8]

Creameries, both private and cooperative, began to buy whole milk in the 1930s, paying the farmer for both the cream that farm families had previously separated at home and the skim milk. After the evening milking, farmers stored the milk in cans; with the morning's milk added, the cans were picked up daily by trucks, thus eliminating a trip to town for the farmer. The creameries separated and processed the product at the plant.[9] Vachon's picture of the woman carrying the milk can illustrates this new, interdependent phase of the dairy industry.

NOTES

1. Here and below, WPA, *Guide to Minnesota,* 68–70 (quotation on 70).

2. D. Jerome Tweton, *Depression: Minnesota in the Thirties* (Fargo: North Dakota Institute for Regional Studies, 1981), 13. The only other area below 12 percent was the Red River valley.

3. Le Sueur, *North Star Country,* 266–67.

4. Tweton, *Depression,* 9; Lee to Stryker, [August] 1937, Stryker Collection.

5. Stryker to Dorothea Lange, September 7, 1939, Stryker Collection; Patricia L. Dooley, "Gopher Ordnance Works: Condemnation, Construction, and Community Response," *Minnesota History* 49 (Summer 1985): 215.

6. David Carmichael, comp., *Guide to the Records of the American Crystal Sugar Company* (St. Paul: Minnesota Historical Society, Division of Archives and Manuscripts, 1985), 3–6.

7. Stryker to Lange, September 30, 1937, Stryker Collection; T. Allen Caine, *Social Life in a Mexican American Community* (San Francisco: R and E Research Associates, 1974), 16, 21, 31–33; Norman S. Goldner, "The Mexican in the Northern Urban Area: A Comparison of Two Generations" (Doctoral diss., University of Minnesota, 1959), 22. On population, see Minnesota, Governor's Interracial Commission, *The Mexican in Minnesota* ([St. Paul], 1948), 9–10, and Susan M. Diebold, "The Mexicans," in *They Chose Minnesota,* ed. Holmquist, 92–96.

8. Lee wrote to Ed Locke, "The wild rice harvesting pictures will have to go — the crop was short and the harvest completed by the time I got to the rice lakes" (September 15, 1937, Stryker Collection). For a study of threshing see J. Sanford Rikoon, *Threshing in the Midwest, 1820–1940: A Study of Traditional Culture and Technological Change* (Bloomington: Indiana University Press, 1988).

9. Pearson, "Dassel," 26–27. A picture of milk cans being unloaded at a cooperative creamery appears in the chapter entitled "Workers in Towns and Cities."

Young Mexican girl topping a sugar beet. East Grand Forks (vicinity). October 1937. *Russell Lee*

OPPOSITE: A Mexican sugar-beet worker's family having coffee after a day's work. East Grand Forks. September 1937. *Russell Lee*

Quarters for housing sugar beet workers during the summer. Chaska (vicinity). September 1937. *Russell Lee*

Mrs. Howard bringing an empty milk can into the home which she and her daughter built on cutover land. Aitkin County. September 1939. *John Vachon*

Loading bags of onions. Rice County. September 1939. *Arthur Rothstein*

Potato worker. East Grand Forks (vicinity). October 1937. *Russell Lee*

Henry Lundgren, manager of the Brandtjen dairy farm, with his wife. Dakota County. September 1939. *Arthur Rothstein*

Milker giving his pet cat milk direct from
the cow on the Brandtjen dairy farm.
Dakota County. September 1939. *Arthur Rothstein*

Cooperative elevator. Sauk Centre. August 1941. *Marion Post Wolcott*

Sign at a grain elevator. Rice [County]. September 1939. *John Vachon*

Indian mother and baby in a blueberry pickers' camp. Little Fork (vicinity). August 1937. *Russell Lee*

An Indian blueberry picker. Little Fork (vicinity). September 1937. *Russell Lee*

Threshing alfalfa seed. Little Fork (vicinity). September 1937. *Russell Lee*

Stacks of wheat and corn. Fergus Falls (vicinity). August 1941. *Marion Post Wolcott*

Child who lives on the other side of the tracks. Minneapolis. September 1939. *John Vachon*

ROADS, RAILS, AND WATERWAYS

THE EARLIEST European visitors traveled by water to Minnesota, using the Great Lakes and their tributaries as highways. In the nineteenth century, settlement followed the rivers — including the nation's major waterway, the Mississippi. Railroads arrived in the North Star State after the Civil War and played a key role in the development of the lumber, iron ore, grain, and flour-milling industries. During the railroad era, the two northern transcontinentals, the Northern Pacific and the Great Northern, established Minneapolis-St. Paul as the gateway to the Pacific Northwest. Ten major trunk lines served the state by the 1930s. With some hyperbole, perhaps, *Minnesota: A State Guide* reported that "twenty-seven railroads crisscross the State in so close a web that scarcely a hamlet is more than 5 miles distant from one or another."[1] Trains, rails, and railroaders persist throughout the Minnesota FSA photographs and provide the context for John Vachon's memorable shot from Minneapolis of the "child who lives on the other side of the tracks."

Motorized vehicles and airplanes were the major innovations in transportation in the twentieth century. Although Minnesota boasted a developing commercial airport at Wold-Chamberlain Field in the Twin Cities and was the home state of Charles A. Lindbergh, Jr., the world's most famous aviator, no photographs of air transportation appear in the file. Instead, the Minnesota pictures show the automobile displacing the railroad as the dominant means of travel. The culture of horse-drawn transportation ended as motorized vehicles came into their own, with automobile and truck registrations increasing from 333,000 in 1921 to more than 800,000 in 1937. Road and highway construction demanded a major share of the budgets of local, state, and federal governments. By the late 1930s, 115,000 miles of secondary roads and 11,000 miles of trunk highways spiderwebbed across Minnesota, including the stretch at Long Siding between Princeton and Milaca. Naturally, unusual vehicles and related equipment occasionally became the subject for the camera. Examples include the truck used by Ojibway blueberry pickers and the snowplow blades at Morris. Unfortunately, the photographers did not take Minnesota pictures of the nation's leading bus company, Greyhound, which began in Hibbing.[2]

Improved road systems made it possible for trucks to emerge as major haulers of raw materials from the country to the city and of finished products and equipment back to the farms and small towns. The old custom of taking a day to drive a wagonload of livestock or produce to market gave way to new relationships, in which individual farmers bought trucks to perform hauling for "regular customers among their neighbors," according to a 1942 observer. Vachon photographed several truckers in the central wholesale district of Minneapolis, including Jack Greaves of Le Sueur. These haulers carried cattle, hogs, grain, lumber, coal, hay — "or anything else which the farmer wishes hauled for a considerable distance" — in their trucks.[3]

Vachon's photographs of Minneapolis pictured other forms of transportation as well. River traffic began expanding in 1939 with the dredging of a nine-foot navigation channel in the

Mississippi, a project authorized by the federal River and Harbor Act of 1930. Locks and dams extended the length of the upper Mississippi from St. Louis, Missouri, to Minneapolis. The streetcars that had been essential to the development of Minneapolis and St. Paul declined in use as cars and buses provided an alternative to the steel tracks girding the metropolitan area. The last trolley in the Twin Cities ran on Hennepin Avenue; it ceased operation in 1954.[4]

Roy Stryker gave specific instructions to Vachon when the St. Paul native returned to Minnesota in the summer of 1941: "You will want to do iron ore and grain since they are the chief things which keep up the work at the Port of Duluth." In his detailed shooting script, Stryker noted that Duluth was a city with 101,000 people. Ships more than six hundred feet long hauled cargoes of 572,000 bushels of wheat or 16,282 tons of coal or iron ore. The boats were loaded by gravity, with the wheat loading at 2,600 bushels per minute and the iron ore at 100 tons per minute. Stryker called for good coverage, saying, "I am personally partial to Duluth."[5]

Vachon took his mother, Ann, with him on his travels to Duluth and the iron ranges. He found Duluth-Superior, which was one of the world's greatest freshwater ports, recovering from the malaise of the depression years, when ore shipments had declined from 50 million tons in 1929 to 2 million tons three years later. By 1941, activity returned to the predepression level. His images of the loading of iron ore were taken primarily in Superior, site of the major iron-ore and coal docks. The twenty-five grain elevators in the Duluth-Superior harbor could store 50 million bushels. Vachon's pictures of grain boats loading are among the finest transportation scenes he photographed. As he described the results to his mother, "The Duluth-Superior pictures are by far the best. They're really very good."[6]

NOTES

1. Here and below, WPA, *Guide to Minnesota,* 81–86 (quotation on 81).

2. Blegen, *Minnesota,* 465; Margaret Walsh, "Tracing the Hound: The Minnesota Roots of the Greyhound Bus Corporation," *Minnesota History* 49 (Winter 1985): 311–12.

3. Pearson, "Dassel," 28–29.

4. St. Paul District, [U.S. Army] Corps of Engineers, *50th Anniversary, Nine-foot Navigation Channel, Upper Mississippi River: Old Man River: 1938–1988* (St. Paul: U.S. Engineer District, [1988]), [3], 6; U.S. Army Corps of Engineers, *The Middle and Upper Mississippi River: Ohio River to Minneapolis,* 2d ed. (Washington, D.C.: Government Printing Office, 1940), 6–7; Stephen A. Kieffer, *Transit and the Twins — A Survey of the History of the Transportation Company in Minneapolis and Saint Paul — An Analysis of the Role of Public Transportation in the Growth of the Twin Cities* ([Minneapolis]: Twin City Rapid Transit Co., 1958), 43–44, 48.

5. Stryker to Vachon, July 15, 18, 1941, Stryker Collection.

6. WPA, *Guide to Minnesota,* 33; Vachon to Mother, [September 1941], Vachon Papers. In a letter to his wife dated September 9, Vachon wrote that he had had his "best day today — loading grain on boats."

Barges on the Mississippi River. The one in the foreground is loaded with wheat for Memphis. Minneapolis.
September 1939. *John Vachon*

A grain elevator. St. Paul.
September 1939. *Arthur Rothstein*

Working [on] the railroad. Minneapolis. September 1939. *John Vachon*

Railroad station waiting room. Morris. September 1939. *John Vachon*

OPPOSITE: Duluth. August 1941. *John Vachon*

Loading a grain boat at the Occident elevator. Duluth. August 1941. *John Vachon*

Grain trimmer. Duluth. August 1941. *John Vachon*

Boat coming in light to take
a load of grain to Buffalo.
Grain elevator superintendent and
sailor's wife waiting in the foreground.
Duluth. August 1941. *John Vachon*

Long Siding. July 1941. .
John Vachon

Snowplows owned by the state highway department. Morris. September 1939. *John Vachon*

Loading truck. Minneapolis. September 1939. *John Vachon*

OPPOSITE: Children of Indian blueberry pickers in a truck. Note the boxes for blueberries and clothes. Little Fork (vicinity). August 1937. *Russell Lee*

Streetcars in a car yard. Minneapolis. September 1939. *John Vachon*

Beer wagon. Minneapolis. September 1939. *John Vachon*

Indian boys playing a guitar and a violin in a blueberry camp. Little Fork (vicinity). September 1937. *Russell Lee*

LEISURE TIME

MINNESOTANS found many ways to enjoy their leisure time. The FSA photographs portray people engaged in a wide variety of activities, such as fishing, camping, hiking, or just relaxing. Unfortunately, the only Minnesota photograph depicting winter sports is John Vachon's image of skaters on Lake Pepin, a place of beauty south of Red Wing where the widened Mississippi River is encircled by towering bluffs. From that same part of the state came Vachon's photograph of a band concert at Kellogg. He also took the Minneapolis picture of a family feeding ducks on the shore of one of the city's many lakes. Russell Lee photographed the Indian boys near Little Fork enjoying a musical break from blueberry picking. The scene of boys fishing at Austin was taken by Paul H. Johnstone, a social scientist employed by the Department of Agriculture.[1]

The St. Paul baseball park, photographed by Russell Lee, was Lexington Park, the home of the St. Paul Saints. This triple-A team competed in the American Association, a league started in 1902. The team's crosstown rival, the Minneapolis Millers, played its games in Nicollet Park. On holidays the teams played doubleheaders, one game in each city, with fans traveling by streetcar between the parks. These were friendly, neighborhood ballparks with green grass under the players' feet and blue sky overhead. Although each had special features — such as the short right field at Nicollet and the presence of the Coliseum Ball Room behind the left field wall at Lexington — neither enjoyed the notoriety of the Hubert H. Humphrey Metrodome in downtown Minneapolis, where the Minnesota Twins played in the 1980s. There, the combination of an artificial surface, inflated dome ceiling, and deafening crowd noise assisted the Twins in bringing Minnesota its first World Series championship in 1987.[2]

In the 1930s and 1940s, before such high-tech mass amusements grabbed the attention of Americans, entertainment came more simply. Indoor activities included motion pictures, ice cream socials, card games, reading, listening to the radio and phonograph, and dancing. Arthur Rothstein took the photograph of the theater at Farmington. Lee provided the striking illustrations of a magazine rack at Cook, a card game at Craigville, an ice cream social at Blackduck, and the 1937 Mexican Independence Day dance.

Tourism was a major hope for Minnesotans, particularly those in the depressed northeast. To counter the negative image conveyed by the term "cutover," other names were proposed for the region — for example, "the playground of the nation" and the more successful "Arrowhead," which was heavily promoted by local boosters. Their enthusiasm was rewarded in 1941 with the publication of the state's second WPA guide. Entitled *The Minnesota Arrowhead Country,* it was written by members of the state's WPA Writers' Program and was included in the American Guide series. The Minnesota Arrowhead Association, Inc., an organization formed in 1923 to promote the region, sponsored the guide. The name "Minnesota Arrowhead Country" had been chosen in a contest that drew thirty thousand entries, the association reported. Noting that few vacation lands could rival the Arrowhead "in sheer diversity of interest," the guide declared that

> the region has everything—rockbound lakes and lakes surrounded by grassy meadows, tranquil and turbulent rivers, hill farms and level plowland, industries large and small, luxuriously appointed summer resorts and isolated beauty spots that are accessible only to the hiker with pup-tent.

Writers noted the scarring of the earth by iron mining but made little mention of the devastation caused by the loggers. Nevertheless, this extensive description of Minnesota presented a compelling case for visiting the Arrowhead country.[3]

Vachon captured many attractions of this region on film, including the Paul Bunyan and Babe the Blue Ox statues at Bemidji. The Rotary Club of Bemidji, in cooperation with the Bemidji Civic and Commerce Association, donated the eighteen-foot statues of the legendary logger and his companion—which were constructed of stucco over steel mesh—in 1937. Babe was originally mounted on a Model T Ford truck and exhibited around the state. Designed to boost tourism, these monuments were another manifestation of the manufactured folk hero of the lumberjacks. Paul Bunyan seems to have been the creation of an advertising agent, William B. Laughead, who worked for the Red River Lumber Company. He wrote his version of the Bunyan stories for customers of the firm in the years after 1914. The photograph of Bunyan was one of Vachon's favorites because the tourist in front is his wife, Penny, who accompanied

him on his trip through northern Minnesota in 1939.[4]

Two other photographs in this chapter were taken by Rothstein on a special assignment in September 1936. Pare Lorentz, a close colleague of Stryker's in the Information Section, was directing a film on the Mississippi River. Rothstein went to Lake Itasca, the headwaters of the great river, to provide shots that would help orient Lorentz and his crew. Rothstein's instructions were "to shoot the terrain as though you were a movie photographer on location . . . with the accent on the Mississippi. There is a marker up that way which shows the source of the Mississippi and Lorentz wants a photograph of that." Many consider the film that resulted, *The River,* to be one of the finest documentaries ever made.[5] Rothstein took other scenes at Itasca State Park. Four years earlier, on the hundredth anniversary of the naming of the headwaters by Henry R. Schoolcraft, citizens presented a historical pageant at the park. It was so successful that the state Department of Conservation, encouraged by business people in Bemidji, Park Rapids, and Bagley, sponsored several weekend pageants there each summer depicting the history of Minnesota. The oxcart pictured is one of the famous Red River carts so important to the early trade and economic life of the territory and state. Ojibway Indians from the Red Lake and White Earth reservations performed in the pageants, which continued, with the exception of the war years, until 1948. Itasca, established in 1891 as a state park, has remained one of the state's most popular tourist attractions.[6]

NOTES

1. Johnstone and Russell Lord were the editors of the 1942 study cited above, *A Place on Earth*.

2. Don Riley (*St. Paul Pioneer Press*), St. Paul, interview with author, December 30, 1987; Dave Mona, comp., *The Hubert H. Humphrey Metrodome Souvenir Book: A Pictorial History of the Twins, Vikings, Gophers, Millers, Saints—and Metrodome!* (Minneapolis: MSP Publications, 1982), 22, 26, 28.

3. Writers' Program, Minnesota, *The Minnesota Arrowhead Country* (Chicago: Albert Whitman and Co., 1941; reprinted as *The WPA Guide to the Minnesota Arrowhead Country,* St. Paul: Minnesota Historical Society Press, 1988), vii (quotations), [232–33]; Landis, *Three Iron Mining Towns,* 51.

4. Writers' Program, *Minnesota Arrowhead Country,* 78, 111,132; Leonard Dickinson, Bemidji, interview with author, January 10, 1988 (Dickinson and his

brother constructed the original statues); Vachon to Penny, July 30, 1941, Vachon Papers; Richard M. Dorson, *America in Legend: Folklore from the Colonial Period to the Present* (New York: Pantheon Books, 1973), 168–70. The most thorough study of the Bunyan tradition in literature is Daniel Hoffman, *Paul Bunyan: Last of the Frontier Demigods* (1952; reprint, Lincoln: University of Nebraska Press, 1983).

5. Stryker to Rothstein, June 6, August 25, 1936, Locke to Rothstein, August 29, 1936, Stryker to Pare Lorentz, February 15, 1937—all in Stryker Collection.

6. John Dobie, *The Itasca Story* (Minneapolis: Ross and Haines, 1959), 110–11; *Farmers Independent* (Bagley), June 27, 1935, p. 1, as found in Ben Thoma, *The Civilian Conservation Corps and Itasca State Park* (Itasca State Park Headquarters, Lake Itasca: C.C.C. History Project, May 1984), 32.

Band concert in the park. Kellogg. July 1941. *John Vachon*

Dance at the Mexican Independence Day celebration. The younger Mexicans are thoroughly Americanized and have retained few of the Mexican customs. St. Paul. September 1937. *Russell Lee*

Skating on the Mississippi River. Lake City (vicinity). February 1942. *John Vachon*

Ice cream social. Blackduck. August 1937. *Russell Lee*

OPPOSITE: A card game in a saloon. Craigville. September 1937. *Russell Lee*

A drugstore display of magazines. Cook. August 1937. *Russell Lee*

OPPOSITE: Motion picture theatre. Farmington. September 1939. *Arthur Rothstein*

Signs and lighting standards at baseball park. St. Paul. August 1937. *Russell Lee*

Boys fishing from piers of dam.
Austin. June 1941. *Paul Johnstone*

175

Family feeding ducks in a park on Saturday afternoon. Minneapolis. September 1939. *John Vachon*

Tourist camp in winter. Minneapolis. November 1937. *John Vachon*

A girl selling pieces of ore and iron range souvenirs to tourists. North Hibbing. August 1941. *John Vachon*

Paul Bunyan monument. Bemidji. September 1939. *John Vachon*

Oxcart used by early
settlers of Minnesota.
Lake Itasca.
August 1936.
Arthur Rothstein

Source of the Mississippi River. Lake Itasca. August 1936. *Arthur Rothstein*

At the home of a Swedish selectee in Minnesota. [Chisago County.] March 1942. *Jack Delano*

WORLD WAR II

AMERICA had been at war for several months when Jack Delano visited Minnesota in the spring of 1942, and by then the need for sacrifice was beginning to be felt in all aspects of American life. At the Historical Section, the staff worried about the agency's survival as the Joint Committee on Nonessential Federal Expenditures, headed by Senator Harry F. Byrd of Virginia, began to question its importance. Roy Stryker described the time as "probably the toughest . . . we have had." To continue its work, the photographic unit had to become "very closely tied to the Coordinator of Information." Through this office FSA photographers were given "special assignments doing pictures of all kinds of stories." Stryker concluded that "the COI is doing a very important [job] of propaganda in the outside and inside of the country and the work is not going to be very much questioned by their brethren on the hill. In the meantime, we will be able to take on a lot of our regular Farm Security work."[1] The COI was one of several agencies consolidated into the Office of War Information in June 1942.

A few weeks before Delano reached the North Star State, John Vachon had taken scenes of selective service registration as he traveled west. President Roosevelt had initiated selective service in September 1940 in response to the dangers posed by the totalitarian regimes of Nazi Germany and the Japanese militarists. Shifting gears to a wartime economy, America prepared reluctantly for international conflict as Dr. New Deal became Dr. Win-the-War.[2] Vachon photographed farmers registering for selective service in west-central Minnesota just weeks after Pearl Harbor. Scenes from Plato, Brownton, and Hutchinson provided dramatic evidence of a people dedicated to the defeat of the Axis aggressors.

The series that Delano took in Minnesota focuses on three Swedish communities in the Chisago Lakes area: Center City, Chisago City, and Lindstrom. Settled in the 1850s, this area of Chisago County was a center of Swedish culture and religion in Minnesota, which people who lived in other states thought of "as the home of the Swedes," according to Stryker. The files for this period contain little correspondence between Stryker and Delano, probably reflecting Stryker's admonition that a new level of "secrecy" was necessary. Delano remembered this assignment as one phase of a project to show what various ethnic groups "were doing in support of the war effort." The OWI wanted these pictures from Minnesota for propaganda purposes related to Sweden, the only Scandinavian country neutral in the war against Germany.[3]

The scenes of the Swedish-American selectees were taken in Center City, which served as the induction center for Chisago County. Pictures show selectees taking the oath of allegiance, being outfitted, and participating in recreational activities. Both the army and the navy are represented. The family pictures offer especially compelling scenes, with grandparents listening to news of the fighting overseas and a father holding a picture of his son. Other photographs depict home-front activities. The Amos and Andy chart, named for the popular radio characters, was used to illustrate the kinds of materials needed to extinguish fires caused by bombs. Although Minnesota was an unlikely target, the deployment of such new weapons as rockets and long-range bombers in Europe made even that remote threat a future possibility. One photograph shows Eric Lind, the postmaster at Chisago City, selling war bonds and defense stamps. Similar activities throughout the state enabled Minnesota to achieve 168 percent of its assigned quota for bond sales.[4] The next year Delano also photographed Sister Elizabeth Kenny, an Australian whose revolutionary techniques for treating polio patients helped free them from the confines of iron lungs. The request for this series came from the OWI office in Australia.[5]

Delano continued with the Swedish theme in Minneapolis, taking pictures of immigrant Arthur Brink, a welder in a war factory, and his wife and one of his four children. Brink, born in Skara, Sweden, was married to the daughter of Swedish immigrants. The photograph demonstrates the censorship that Swedish families experienced during the war.[6] The image of women baking cookies for servicemen helps to show the totality of the war effort. Delano's creative photograph of the Swedish worker at the Northern Pump Company in Minneapolis is one of a series taken at that plant. With its subsidiary, Northern Ordnance, Northern Pump was the largest producer of ordnance for the U.S. Navy during World War II. The Minneapolis plant manufactured gun mounts, power drives for aircraft carrier elevators, and vibration dampers for submarines.[7]

Minnesota shared in the pride and the sorrow of World War II. According to historian Virginia B. Kunz, a Minnesota naval reserve unit serving on the destroyer USS *Ward* fired the first American shot of the war, scoring a direct hit on a Japanese submarine at Pearl Harbor. The state sent 304,000 men off to war, of whom more than 6,000 lost their lives in the nation's defense.[8] Those who returned came home to a state quite different from the one they had left. Most likely, they were unaware as they boarded the troop trains and ships that they had taken a last look at their homeland "as it used to be."

NOTES

1. Stryker to Rothstein, February 17, 1942, Stryker to Lee, March 18, 1942, both in Stryker Collection. Stryker told Lee that his first job for the COI was to take pictures of "Swedish American actors and actresses taking part in Civil Defense activities. Greta Garbo knitting for the Red Cross, etc." This letter provides further evidence supporting the explanation presented here regarding Delano's assignment in Minnesota.

2. President Roosevelt used this description in response to a reporter's question. See "The Nine Hundred and Twenty-ninth Press Conference (Excerpts), December 28, 1943," in *The Public Papers and Addresses of Franklin D. Roosevelt,* comp. Samuel I. Rosenman, *1943 Volume* (New York: Harper and Brothers, 1950), 569–71.

3. Stryker to Lee, March 18, 1942, Stryker Collection; Jack Delano to author, January 10, 1988.

4. Notes from Delano's personal files indicate that Lind came to the United States in 1898 at the age of twenty-six from Kelefors, Heligoland (probably Kilafors, Hälsingland: see obituary in *Chisago County Press* [Lindstrom], August 12, 1948, p. 1). The three elderly Swedes listening to the radio are Christine Dahlsten (eighty-eight years old, from Rättvik, Dalarna), Emma Eastland (eighty-three years old, from Kronobergs Län, Småland), and David Petersen (seventy-five years old, from Linneryd, Småland) (Delano to author, January 10, 1988). Highlights of Minnesota's involvement in World War II are discussed in Blegen, *Minnesota,* 541–49.

5. Stryker to Minneapolis General Hospital, January 29, 1943, FSA-OWI Correspondence. The world-famous Sister Kenny Institute became a part of Abbott Northwestern Hospital, Minneapolis, in 1975. Kenny's story is told in Victor Cohn, *Sister Kenny: The Woman Who Challenged the Doctors* (Minneapolis: University of Minnesota Press, 1975).

6. Information from caption for photograph LC-USW 3-9970, FSA-OWI Collection.

7. Joseph Stipanovich, *City of Lakes: An Illustrated History of Minneapolis* (Woodland Hills, Calif.: Windsor Publications, 1982), 348–49.

8. Virginia Brainard Kunz, *Muskets to Missiles: A Military History of Minnesota* (St. Paul: Minnesota Statehood Centennial Commission, 1958), 170–72, 182.

Selective service registration. Hutchinson. February 1942. *John Vachon*

Selective service registration for men 20–44, not previously registered. Brownton. February 1942. *John Vachon*

Farmer registering for selective service. Plato. February 1942. *John Vachon*

Swedish-American selectee in Minnesota
being inducted into the U.S. Navy.
[Center City.] April 1942. *Jack Delano*

Swedish-American selectees in Minnesota taking the oath as they are inducted into the U.S. Army. [Center City.] April 1942. *Jack Delano*

Swedish-American selectee of Minnesota receiving issue of clothing as he is inducted into the U.S. Army. [Center City.] April 1942. *Jack Delano*

Swedish-American selectee from the State of Minnesota, just inducted into the U.S. Army, enjoying a bit of recreation.
[Center City. April 1942.] *Jack Delano*

A Swedish postmaster in a small Minnesota town selling defense bonds to Swedish farmers. [Chisago City.]
April 1942. *Jack Delano*

Fire department official in a small Minnesota town instructing Swedish-American civilian defense fire spotters with a diagram of an incendiary bomb. [Chisago County.] April 1942. *Jack Delano*

Sister Kenny conducting a class for technicians at the Elizabeth Kenny Institute. Minneapolis. February 1943. *Jack Delano*

Mr. Brink receives frequent letters from his relatives in Sweden. This one has been stamped "Geoeffnet" — opened by the German censor. Minneapolis. March 1942. *Jack Delano*

The father of a Swedish-American
selectee from Minnesota
in the U.S. Army.
[Chisago County.]
April 1942. *Jack Delano*

Women of Swedish extraction, members of a church group, baking cookies for a servicemen's center. Minneapolis. March 1942. *Jack Delano*

A defense worker who was born in
Sweden welding at a plant in Minnesota,
possibly the Northern Pump Company
in Minneapolis. April 1942. *Jack Delano*

LIBRARY OF CONGRESS NEGATIVE NUMBERS

The photographs in this book are on file in the Prints and Photographs Division of the Library of Congress, Washington, D.C. Negative numbers for the photographs are listed here by order of the page on which they appear.

ii	LC-USF 34-64470-D	47	LC-USF 34-63364-D	89	LC-USF 34-30162-E
v	LC-USF 341-11170-B	48	LC-USF 33-1489-M5	90	LC-USF 33-11352-M4
2	LC-USF 34-64606-D	49	LC-USF 34-63328-D	91	LC-USF 34-30035-E
5	LC-USF 33-16019-M1	50	LC-USF 33-1639-M1	92	LC-USF 33-11269-M3
7	LC-USF 33-1445-M5	54	LC-USF 33-1645-M5	93	LC-USF 33-11353-M2
10	LC-USF 34-63325-D	55	LC-USF 33-15558-M5	94	LC-USF 33-11270-M4
14	LC-USF 34-30641-D	56	LC-USF 33-1509-M1	95	LC-USF 34-30683-D
15	LC-USF 33-11342-M3	57	LC-USF 33-1643-M2	96	LC-USF 34-30686-D
16	LC-USF 33-11344-M3	58	LC-USF 34-30025-E	97	LC-USF 34-30691-D
17	LC-USF 33-11348-M4	59	LC-USF 33-1556-M3	98	LC-USF 34-30689-D
18	LC-USF 34-30609-D	60	LC-USF 34-60309-D	99	LC-USF 33-11346-M5
19	LC-USF 34-30613-D	61	LC-USW 3-991-D	100	LC-USF 342-30632-A
20	LC-USF 34-30268-D	62	LC-USF 33-1586-M1	101	LC-USF 34-30318-D
21	LC-USF 33-11276-M1	63	LC-USF 34-60331-D	102	LC-USF 34-30584-D
22	LC-USF 33-1500-M2	64	LC-USF 34-57807-D	103	LC-USF 34-30587-D
23	LC-USF 33-15555-M4	65	LC-USF 33-1665-M5	104	LC-USF 34-30390-D
24	LC-USF 33-11272-M5	66	LC-USF 33-1548-M1	107	LC-USF 34-30285-D
25	LC-USF 34-30581-E	67	LC-USF 33-1464-M2	108	LC-USF 342-30496-A
26	LC-USF 33-11301-M4	68	LC-USF 34-30666-D	109	LC-USF 34-63911-D
27	LC-USF 33-1477-M2	69	LC-USF 33-1636-M3	110	LC-USF 34-63916-D
28	LC-USF 34-30282-D	70	LC-USF 33-1638-M2	111	LC-USF 34-64024-D
29	LC-USF 34-30425-D	71	LC-USF 33-16035-M2	112	LC-USF 34-63930-D
30	LC-USF 33-1494-M1	72	LC-USF 33-1591-M5	113 (left)	LC-USF 34-63982-D
34	LC-USF 34-60251-D	75 (left)	LC-USF 34-60402-D	113 (right)	LC-USF 34-63931-D
35	LC-USF 341-11168-B	75 (right)	LC-USF 34-60407-D	114	LC-USF 34-63848-D
36	LC-USF 341-11167-B	76	LC-USF 34-60414-D	115	LC-USF 34-64048-D
37	LC-USF 341-11184-B	77	LC-USF 34-60343-D	116	LC-USF 34-64451-D
38	LC-USF 33-1474-M2	78	LC-USF 33-1611-M5	120	LC-USF 34-61764-D
39	LC-USF 341-11177-B	79	LC-USF 33-1517-M3	121	LC-USF 34-61765-D
40	LC-USF 341-11244-B	80	LC-USF 34-63299-D	122	LC-USF 34-64467-D
41	LC-USF 341-11251-B	81	LC-USF 34-63296-D	123	LC-USF 34-64452-D
42	LC-USF 34-60321-D	82	LC-USF 34-63351-D	124	LC-USF 34-64443-D
43	LC-USF 34-60323-D	83	LC-USF 33-1490-M2	125 (left)	LC-USF 34-61416-D
44	LC-USF 34-60319-D	84	LC-USF 34-60243-D	125 (right)	LC-USF 34-64461-D
45	LC-USF 34-63406-D	85	LC-USF 33-11299-M2	126	LC-USF 34-61433-D
46	LC-USF 34-63365-D	86	LC-USF 33-11352-M2	127	LC-USF 34-64583-D

THIS BOOK WAS SET IN SABON TYPE AND PAGES WERE MADE UP ON A COMPUGRAPHIC
SYSTEM AT PEREGRINE PUBLICATIONS. THE PHOTOGRAPHS WERE REPRODUCED
AS 200-LINE-SCREEN DUOTONES IN BLACK AND WARM GRAY INKS. VIKING PRESS PRINTED
THE BOOK ON WARREN'S LUSTRO DULL STOCK. BOTH CLOTH AND PAPERBACK
BOOKS, WHICH WERE BOUND BY MIDWEST EDITIONS, ARE SMYTH SEWN FOR DURABILITY.
ALAN OMINSKY DESIGNED THE COVER AND INTERIOR.